Table of Contents

CLAIM YOUR FREE BONUS GIFT!

As our way of saying thank you for your purchase, we want to give you a **very special gift** to help you in your scrapbooking.

To get your FREE gift from us, just visit this special page on our website:

www.scrapbookingcoach.com/gift

Hi and welcome to 525 New & Inspiring Scrapbooking Sketches!

I'm Anna Lyons, founder of Scrapbooking Coach.com

If you've ever struggled with scrappers block, how to start a layout or have lost the confidence to scrap, then this book will transform your scrapbooking.

Using sketches is fun and EASY and they can save you time and give you lots of quick inspiration. And sketches also leave lots of room for your own creativity too…

You see, a sketch simply tells you what goes where. And anyone who's spent hours and hours pushing things around on a page knows how important that is.

But outside of the page plan, what color of card stock and embellishments you use is entirely up to you!

In fact, you could use the same sketch to create two totally different pages (just by choosing dif-ferent colored and textured paper / embellishments).

Cool huh?

Before I forget, I also want to encourage you to print out your copy of 525 New And Inspiring Scrapbooking Sketches so you always have a hard copy. Stick it in a binder or staple it together. It's great to have lying round the place, so you can just flick through a few pages and get in-spired.

Feel free to take 525 New And Inspiring Scrapbooking Sketches to your next crop too!

I really hope you enjoy the inspiration and ideas within, and I wish you nothing but fun and ex-citement with your scrapbooking

Also – if you have any feedback or perhaps a testimonial about how 525 New And Inspiring Scrapbooking Sketches has helped you, I would love to hear from you.

Please email me personally – support@scrapbookingcoach.com
Be inspired to creatively preserve your most precious memories, now and always.

Anna Lyons

Anna Lyons
Scrapbookingcoach.com

How to Use 525 New & Inspiring Scrapbooking Sketches!

Each chapter inside 525 New And Inspiring Scrapbooking Sketches showcases sketches by amount of photos.

Let's say for example you have 3 photos, simply select the chapter that has sketches with 3 photos or more! Then browse the chapter until you find a sketch that you like.

Once you've found a sketch, prepare your stash so you have all the necessary page elements. Then when you're ready to build your layout just adhere each element to your according to the sketch.

For example if, your photo has a matte, adhere the matte to your page first and THEN the photo on top.

Then build the layers up and watch your page come to life!

Use this sketch...

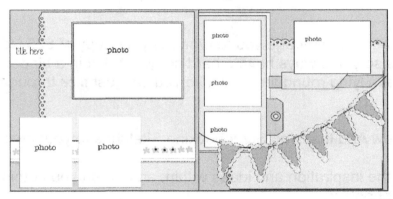

...To create this gorgeous page!

The Two Ways To Use 525 New And Inspiring Scrapbooking Sketches

There's two ways we encourage scrappers to use our sketches.

1. Copy each sketch exactly to guarantee a perfect layout every time…

Or…

2. Tweak and adjust each sketch as you please to create your masterpiece.

Either way is fine!

Most scrappers start by copying our sketches, but after a while, something amazing tends to happen…

Your own creativity blossoms, and before long you'll be adding your own personal touch to each sketch!

And with the many ways you can tweak, the 525 sketches become 5250 sketches!

One Photo Sketches

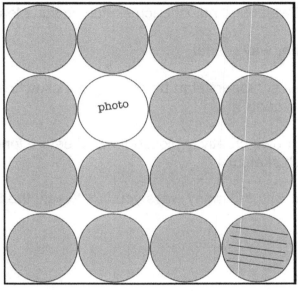

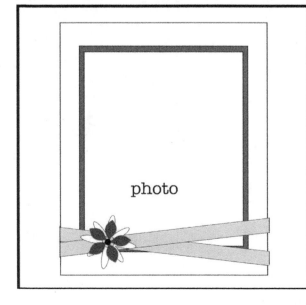

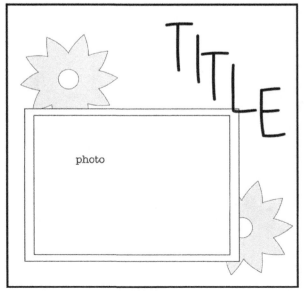

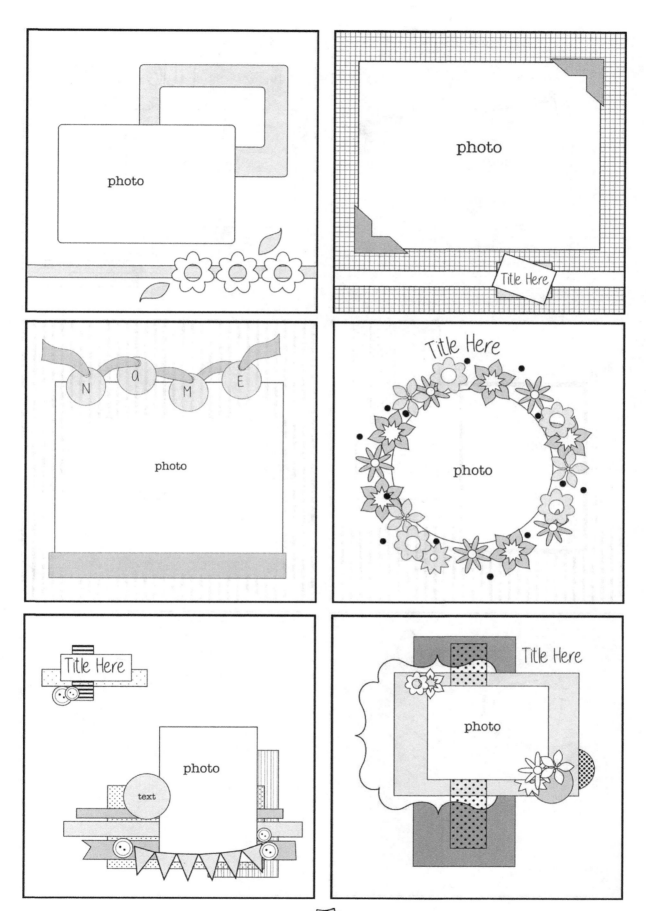

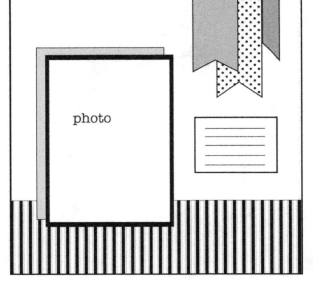

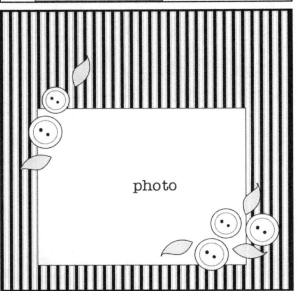

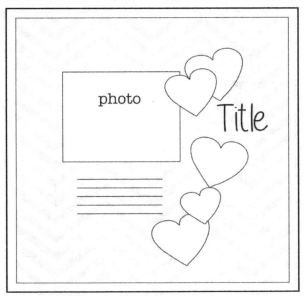

9

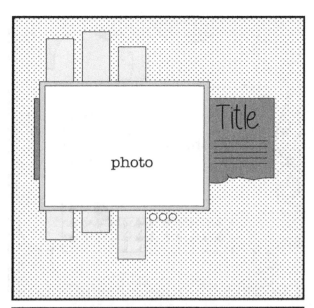

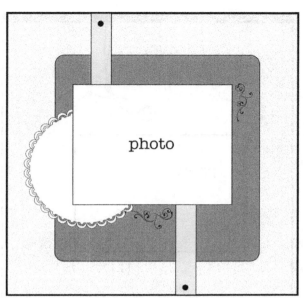

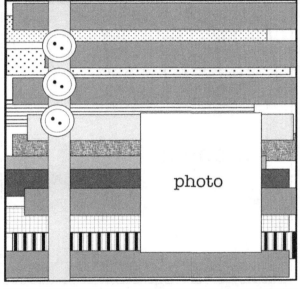

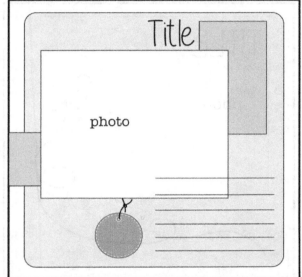

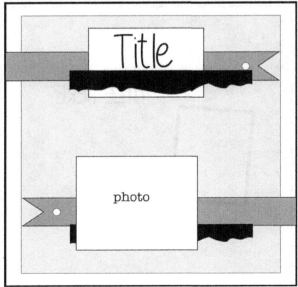

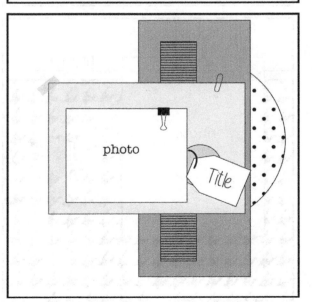

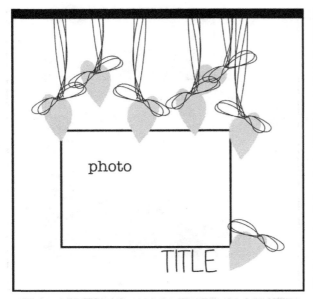

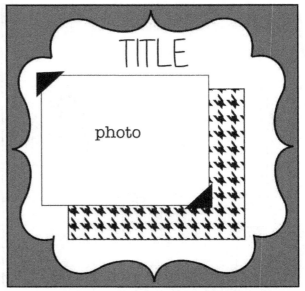

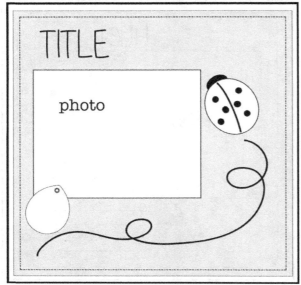

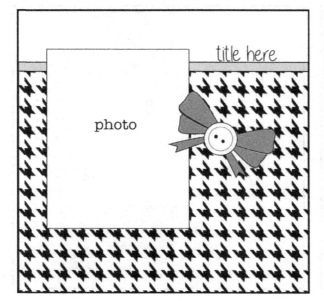

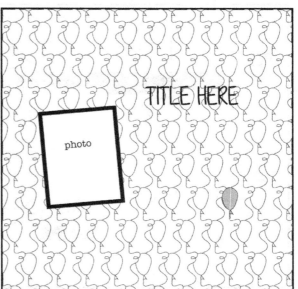

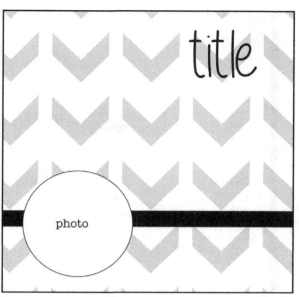

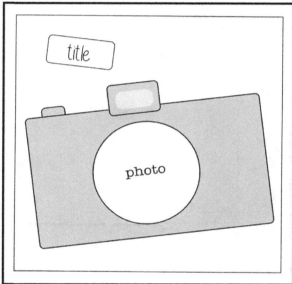

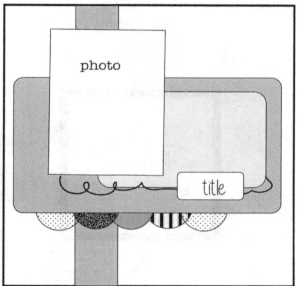

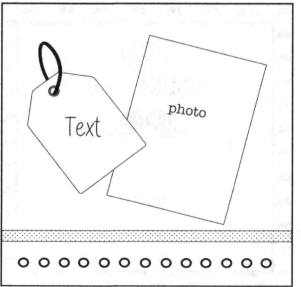

photo

title here

title here

photo

title

photo

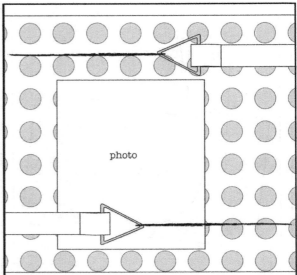

photo

Title
subtitle here

photo

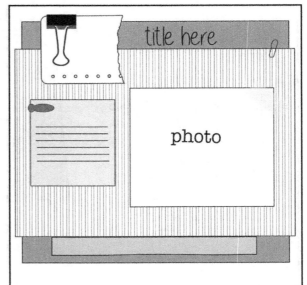

title here

photo

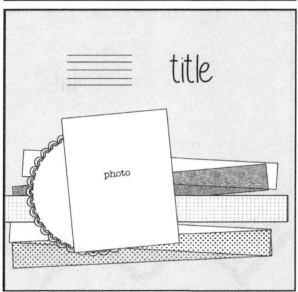

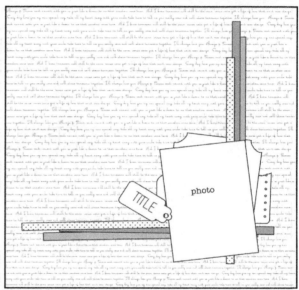

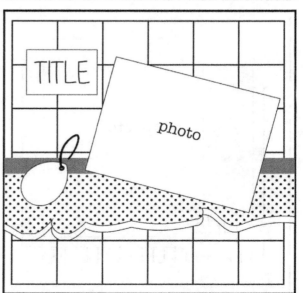

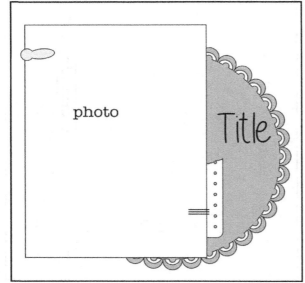

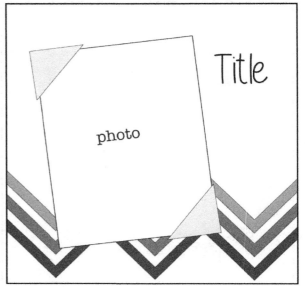

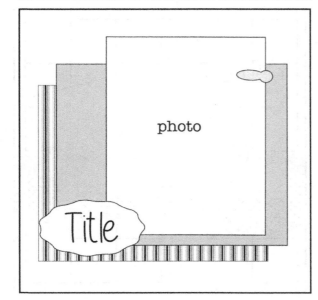

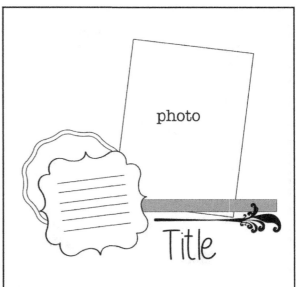

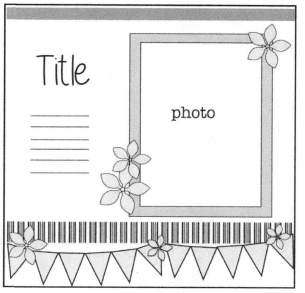

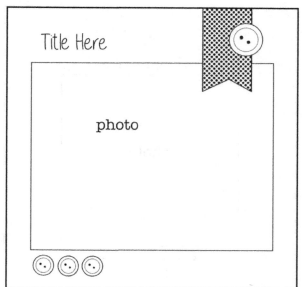

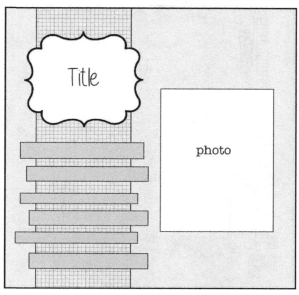

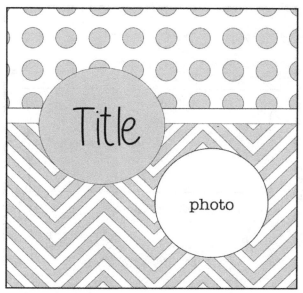

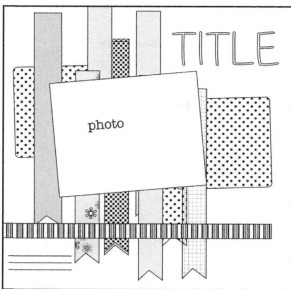

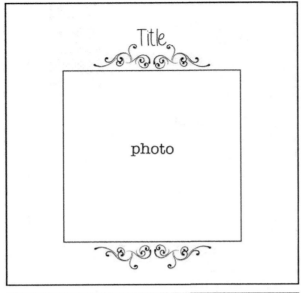

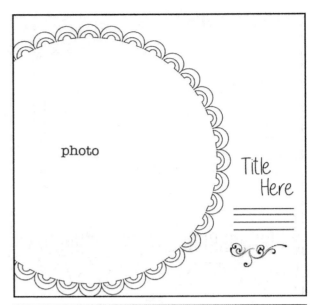

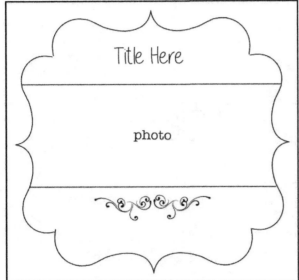

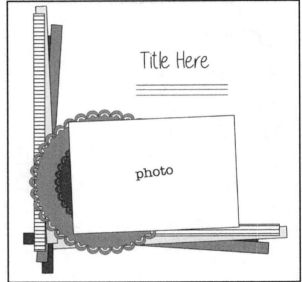

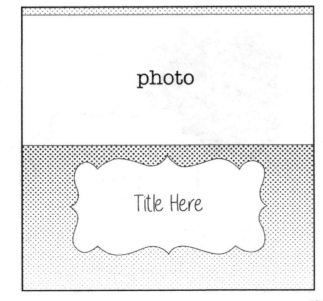

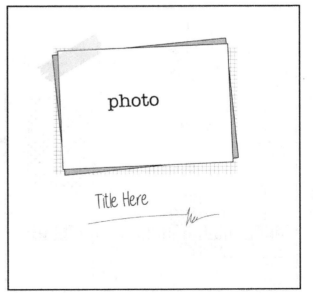

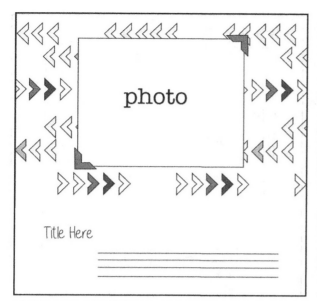

Title Here

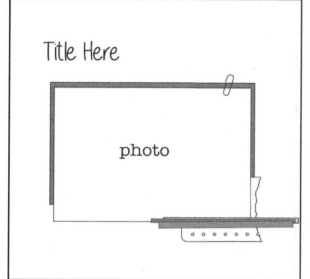

Title Here

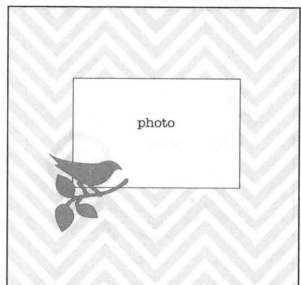

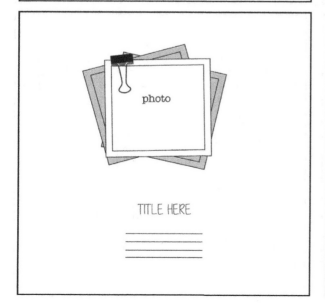

TITLE HERE

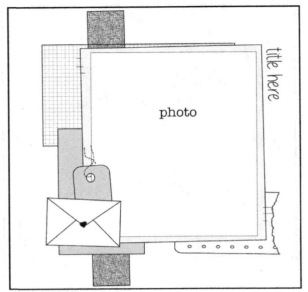

title here

photo

title here

photo

title here

photo

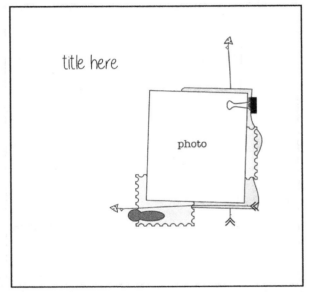

title here

photo

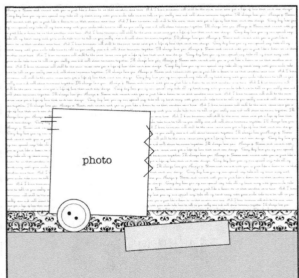

photo

photo

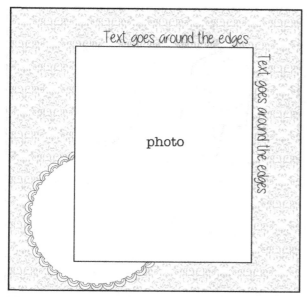

Text goes around the edges

Text goes around the edges

photo

title here

photo

title here

photo

title

photo

title

photo

Title Here

photo

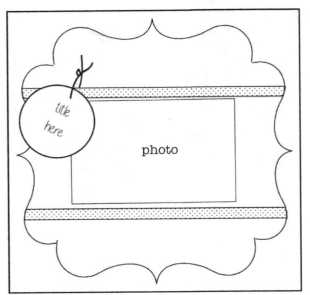

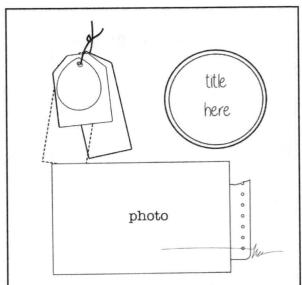

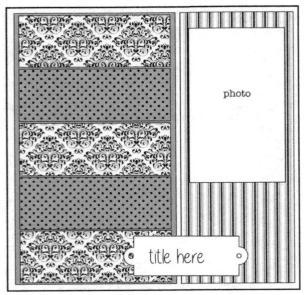

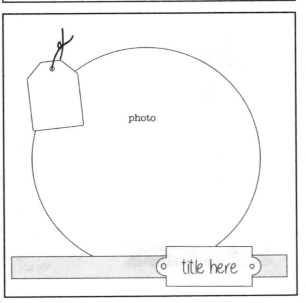

photo

title here
Subtitle Here

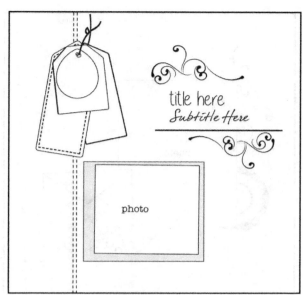

title here
Subtitle Here

photo

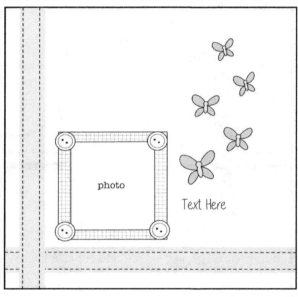

photo

Text Here

title here

photo

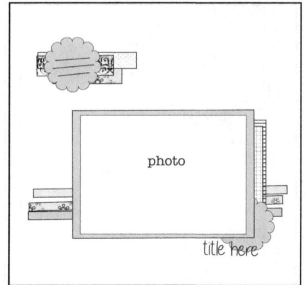

photo

title here

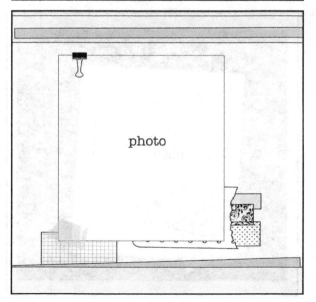

photo

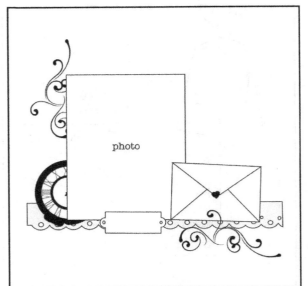

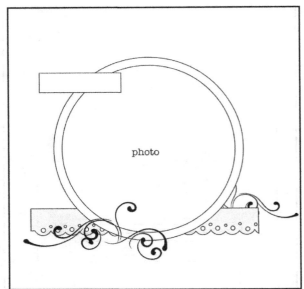

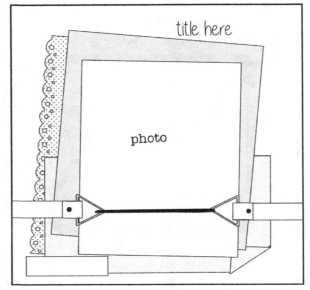

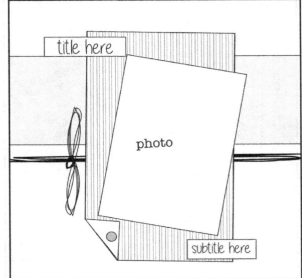

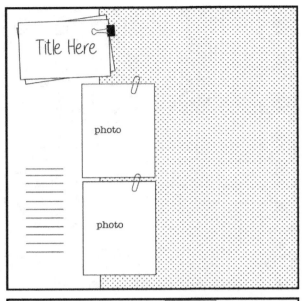

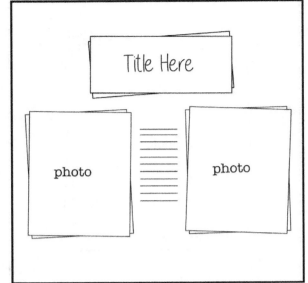

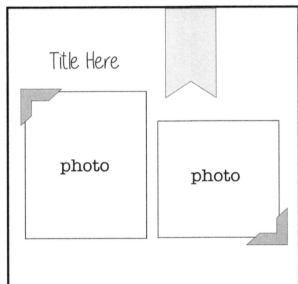

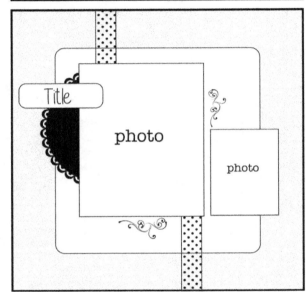

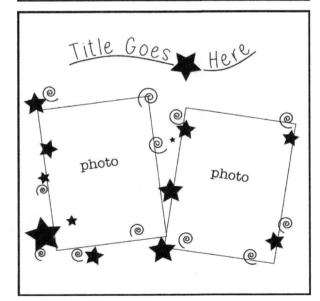

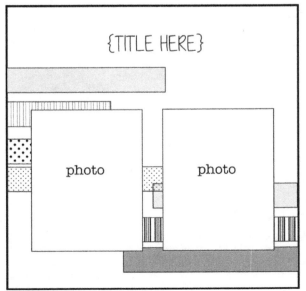

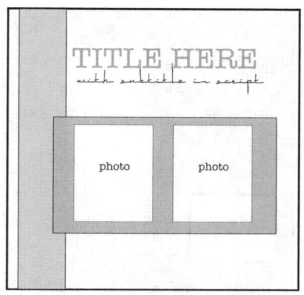

TITLE HERE
with subtitle in script

Title Here

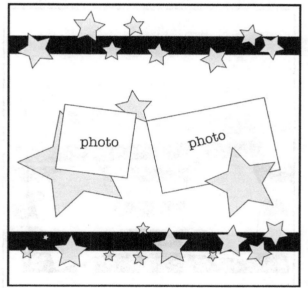

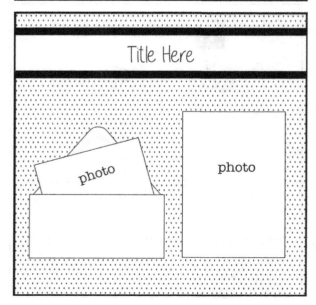

Title Here

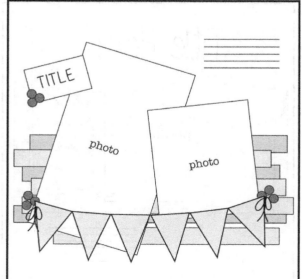

TITLE

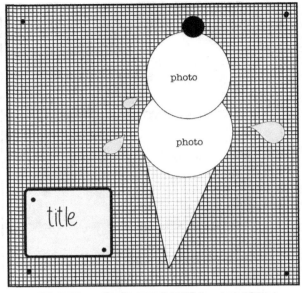

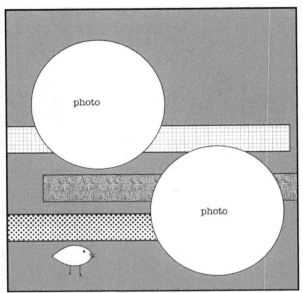

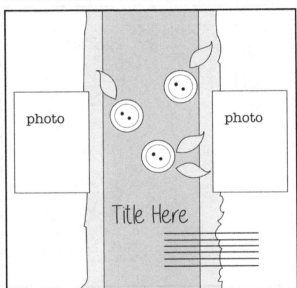

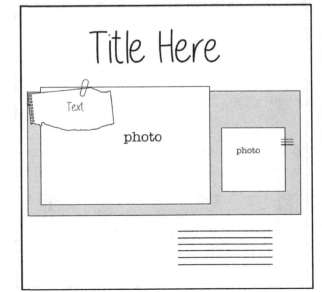

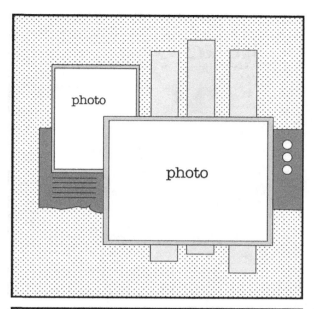

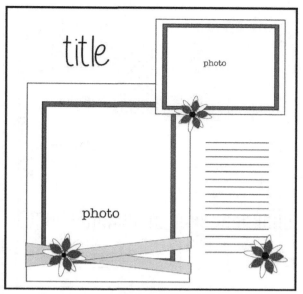

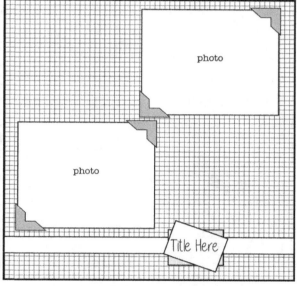

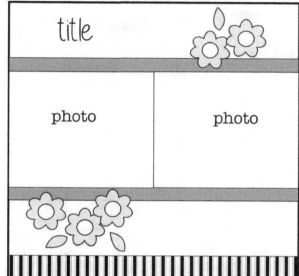

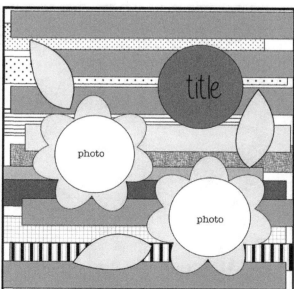

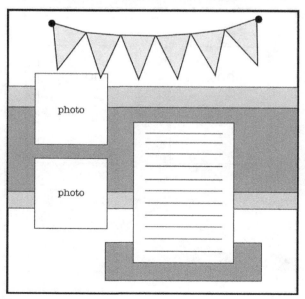

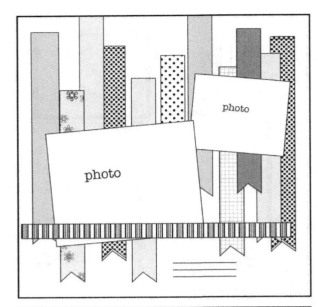

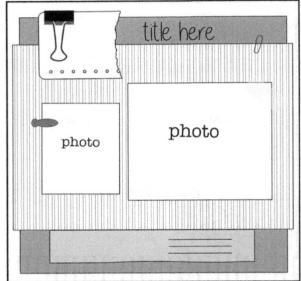

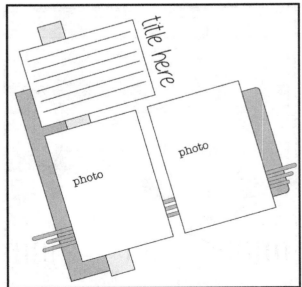

29

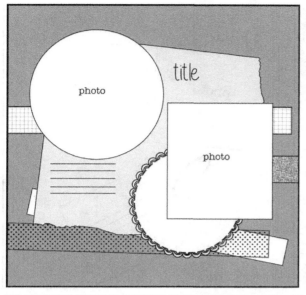

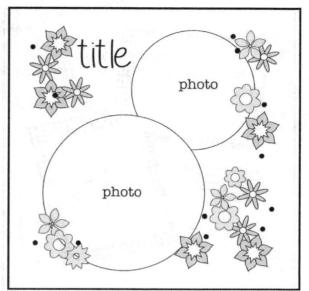

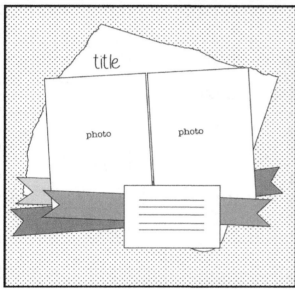

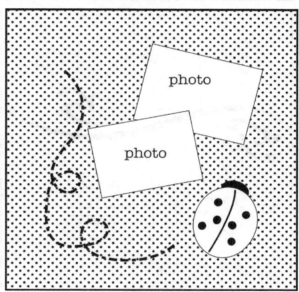

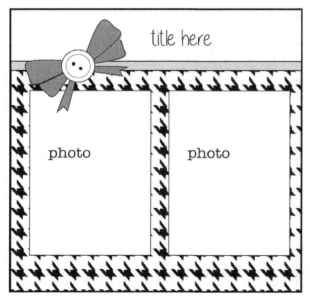

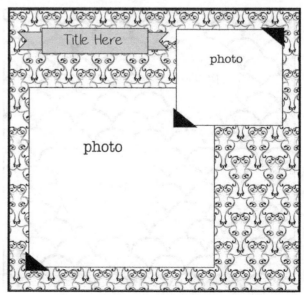

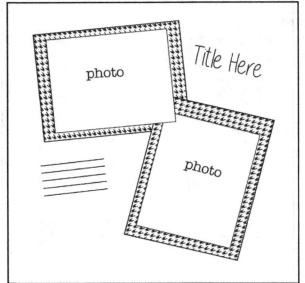

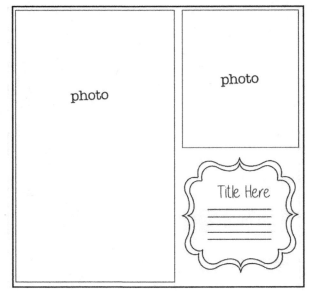

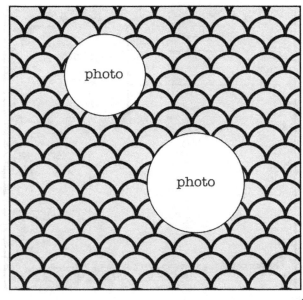

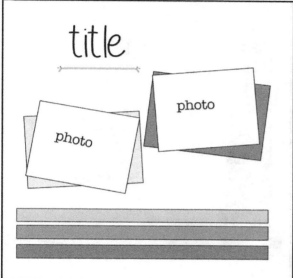

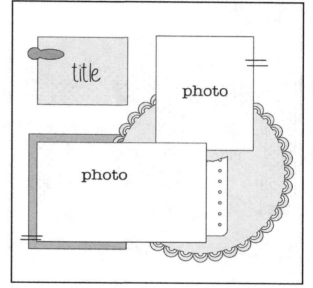

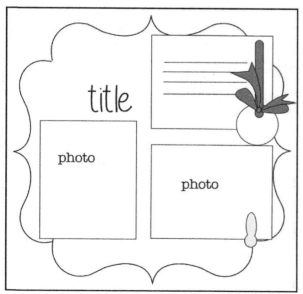

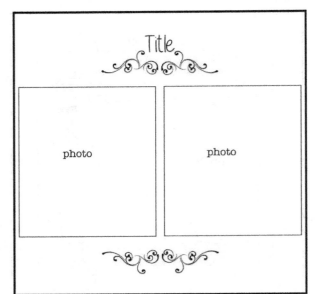

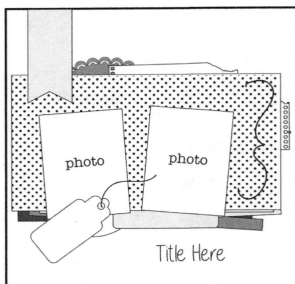

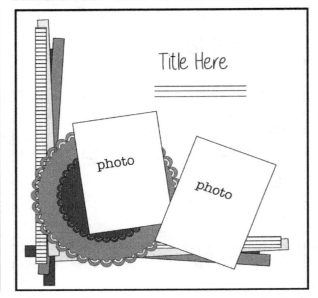

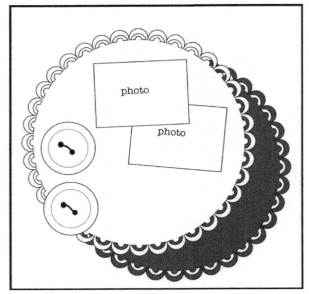

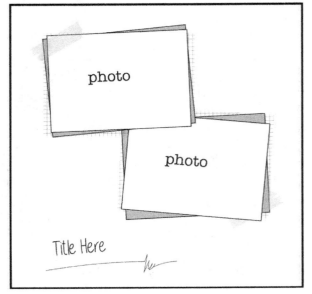

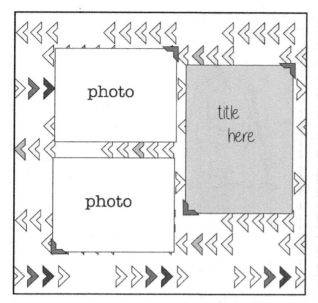

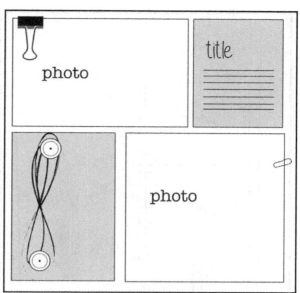

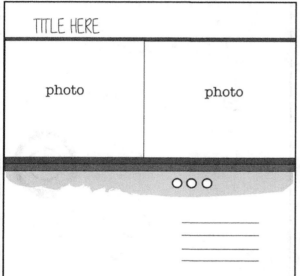

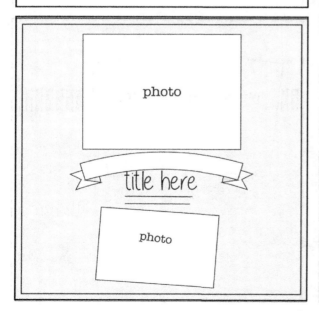

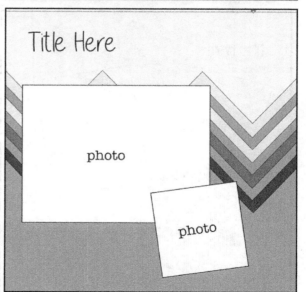

photo

photo

title here

title here
Subtitle Here

photo

photo

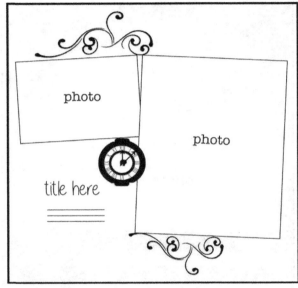

photo

photo

title here

title here

photo

photo

title here

photo

photo

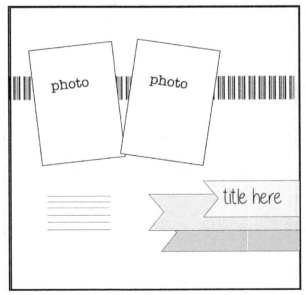

photo

photo

title here

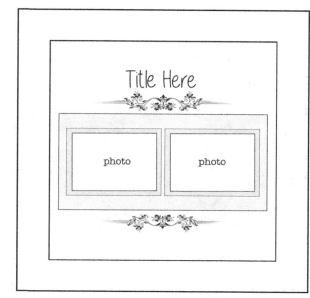

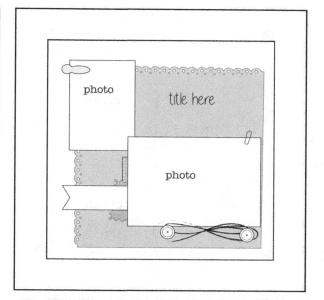

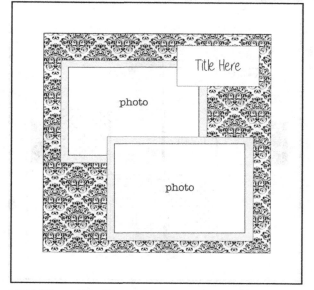

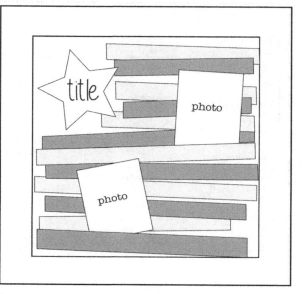

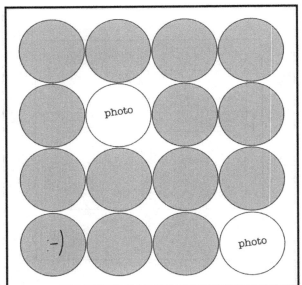

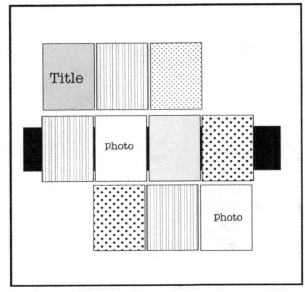

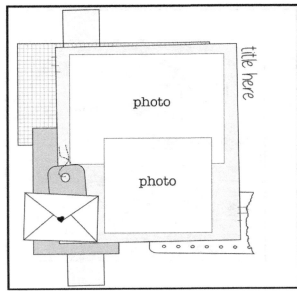

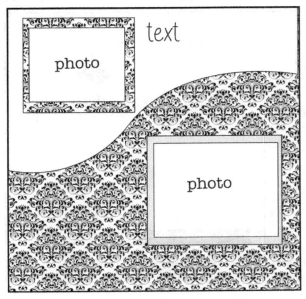

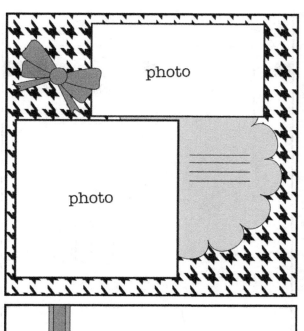

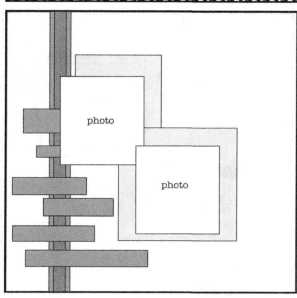

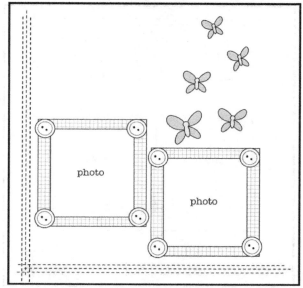

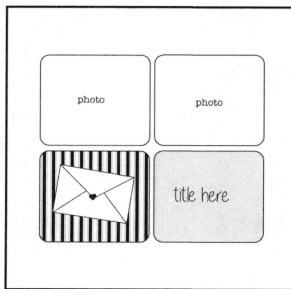

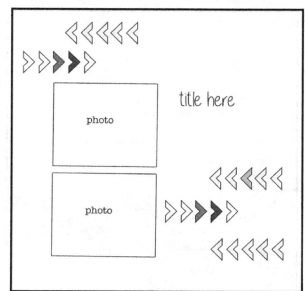

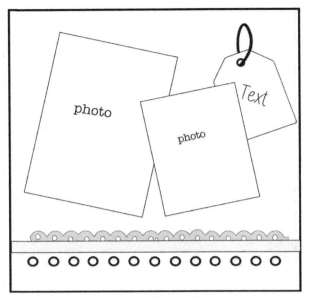

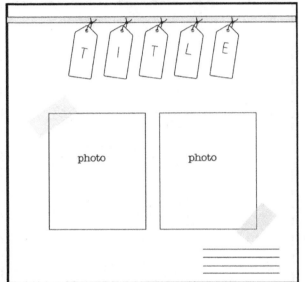

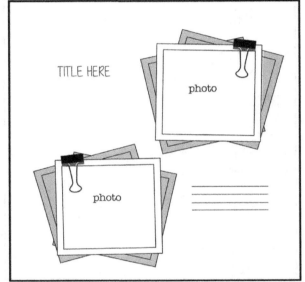

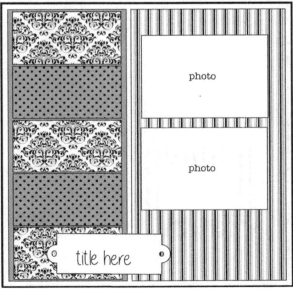

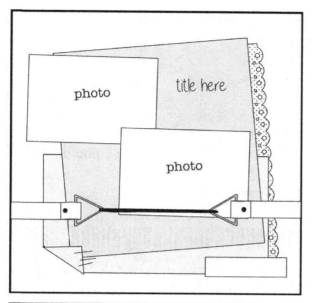

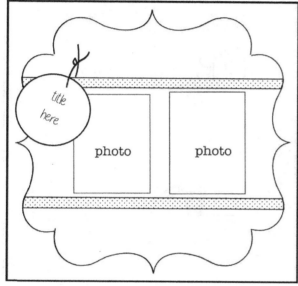

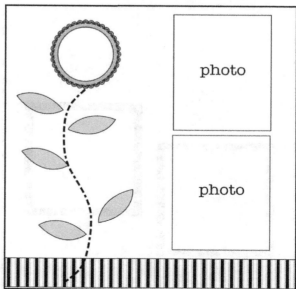

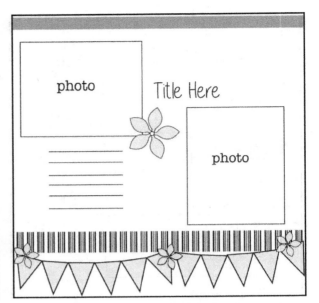

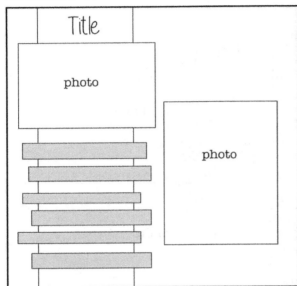

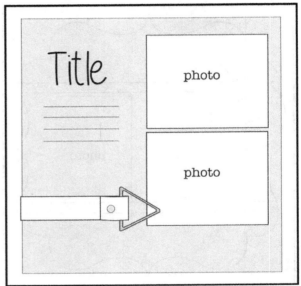

photo

photo

title here

TITLE HERE

photo

photo

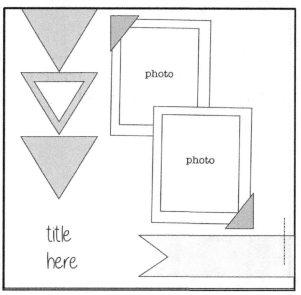

photo

photo

title here

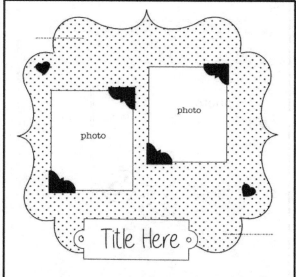

photo

photo

Title Here

Three Photo Sketches

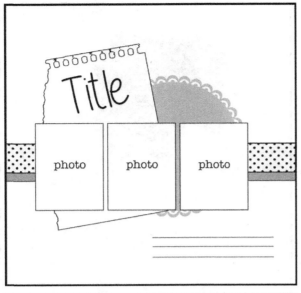

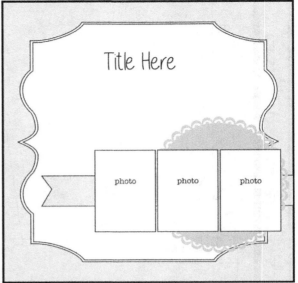

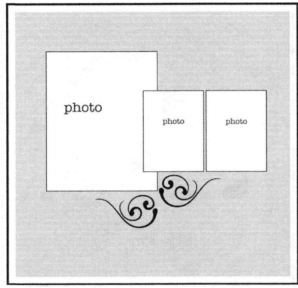

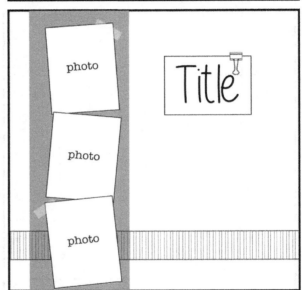

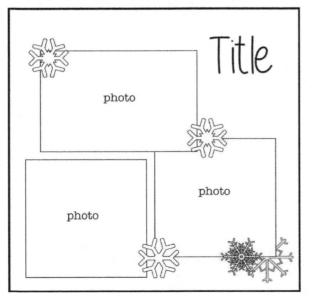

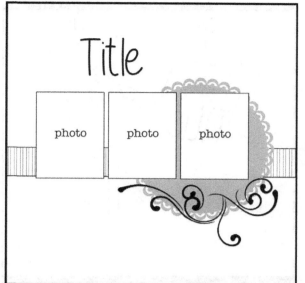

Title

photo photo photo

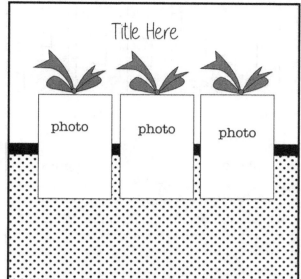

Title Here

photo photo photo

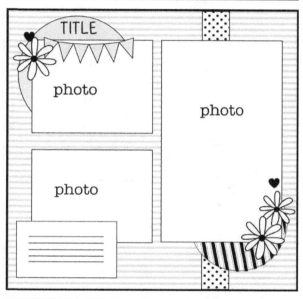

TITLE

photo

photo

photo

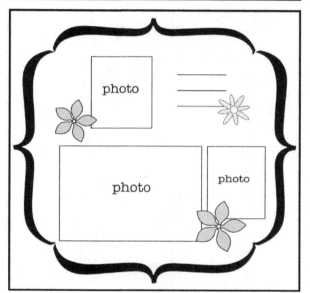

photo

photo photo

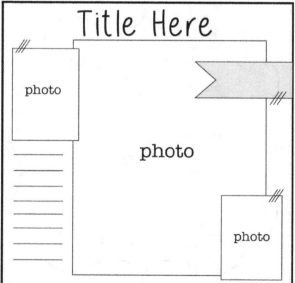

Title Here

photo

photo

photo

Title Here

photo

photo

photo

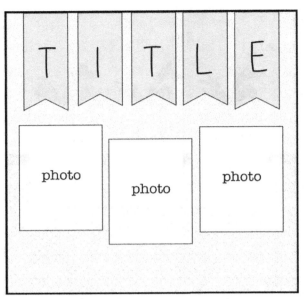

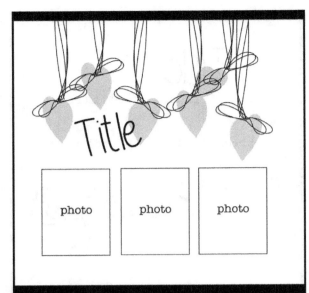

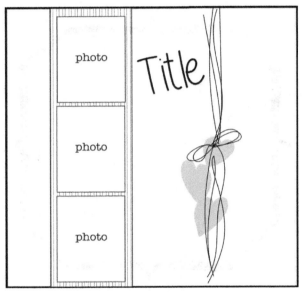

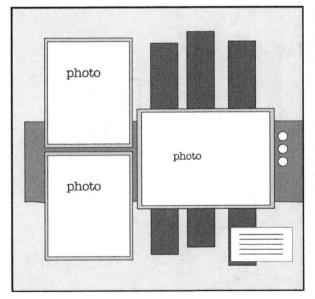

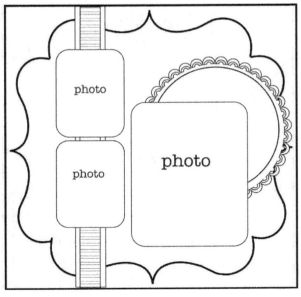

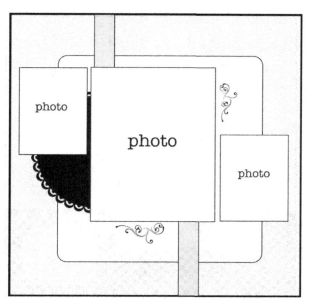

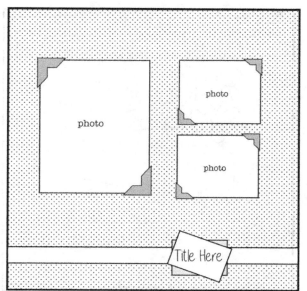

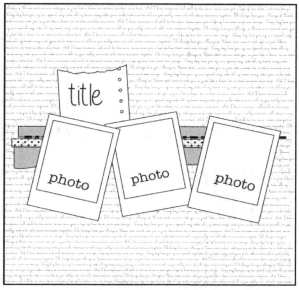

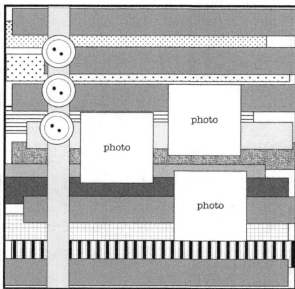

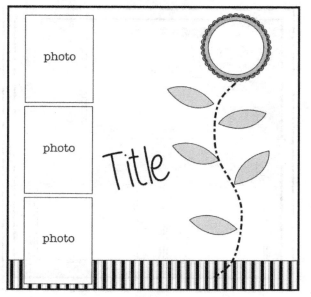

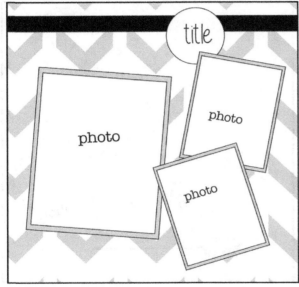

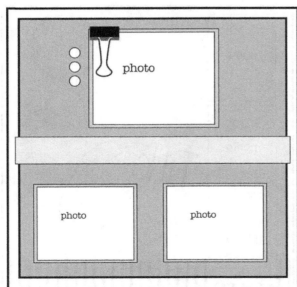

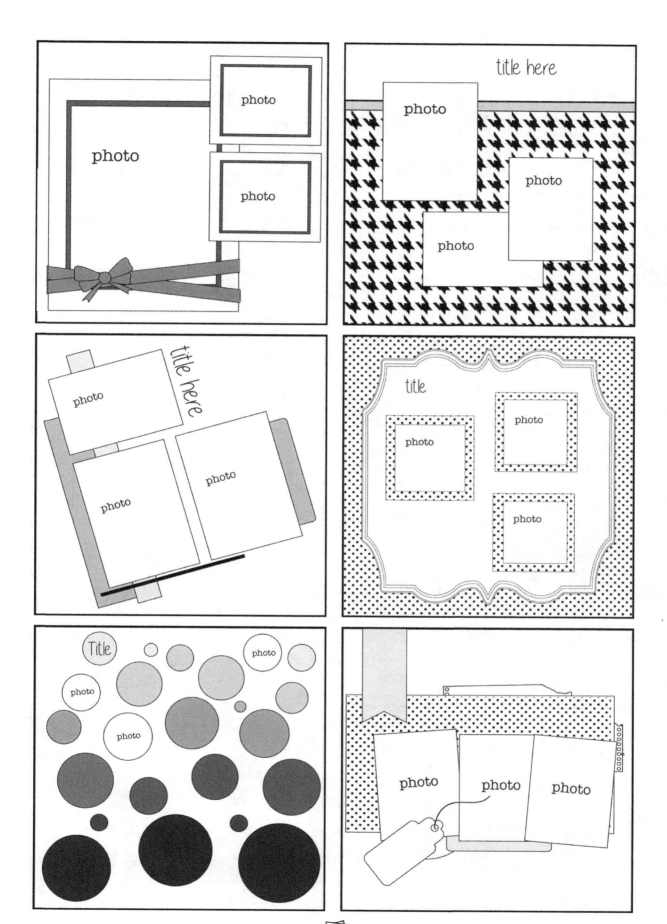

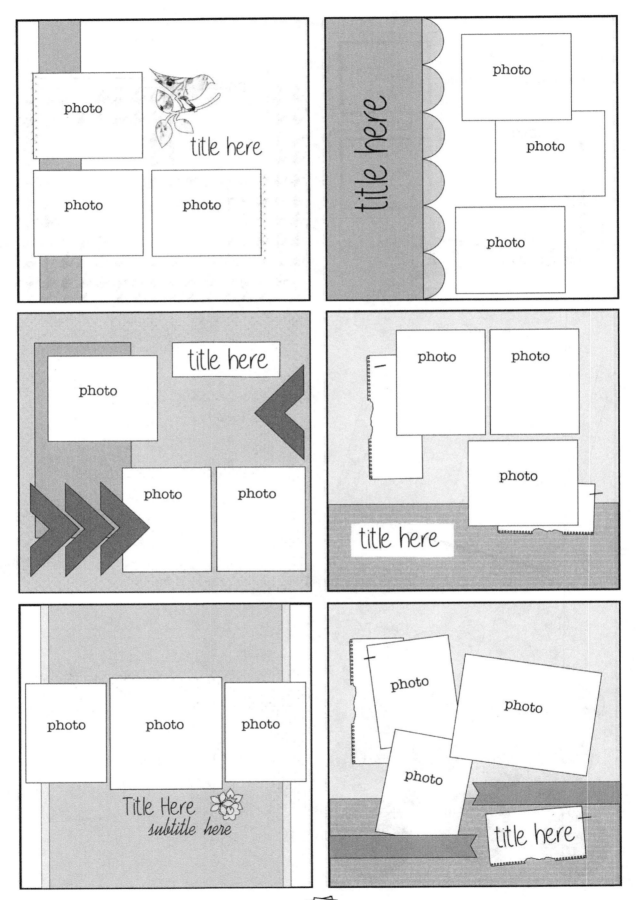

title here

photo

photo

photo

title here

photo

photo

photo

title here

photo

photo

photo

photo

photo

photo

title here

photo

photo

photo

Title Here
subtitle here

photo

photo

photo

title here

49

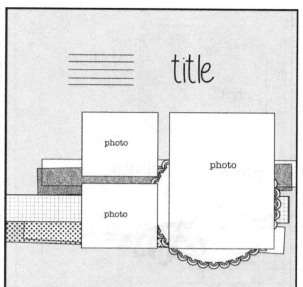

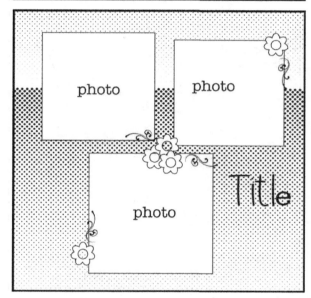

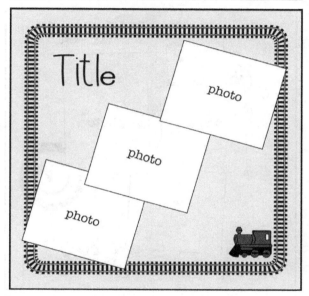

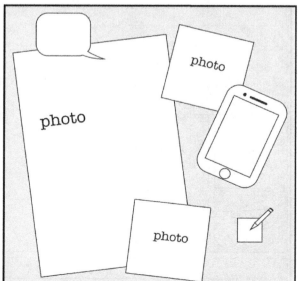

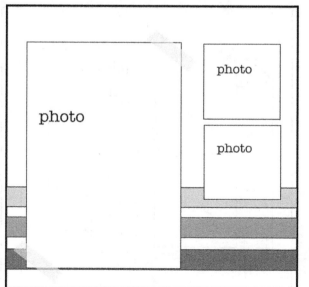

title here

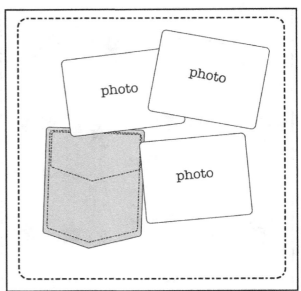

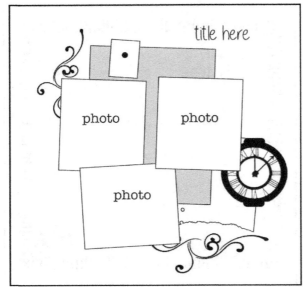

title here

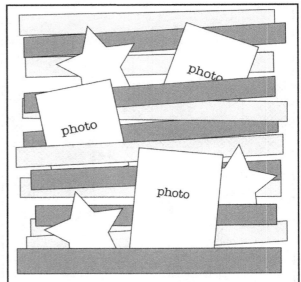

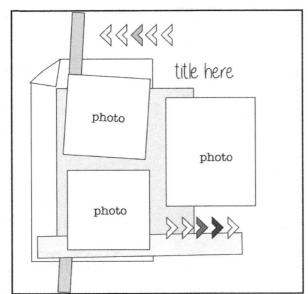

title here

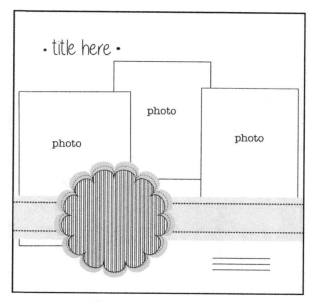

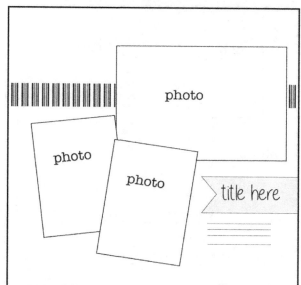

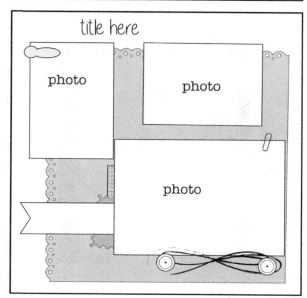

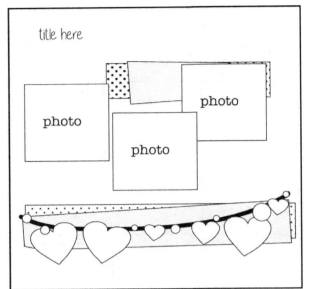

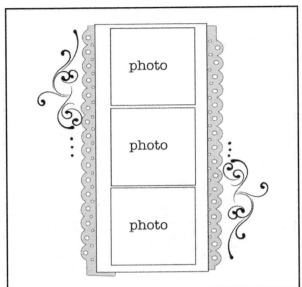

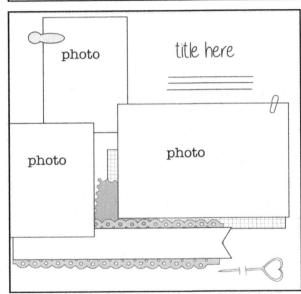

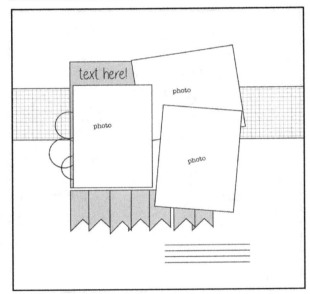

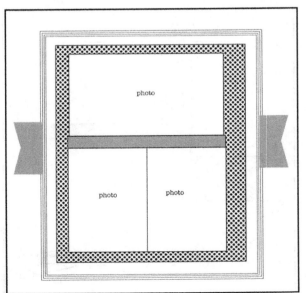

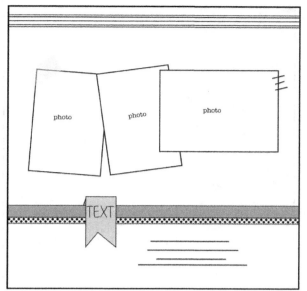

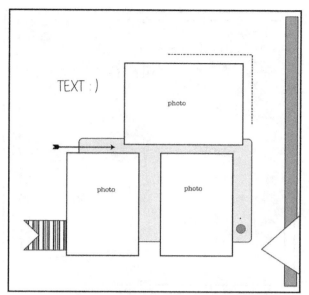

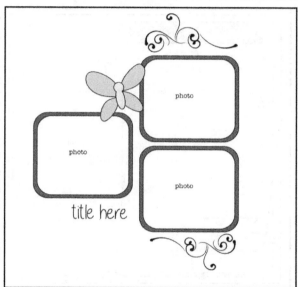

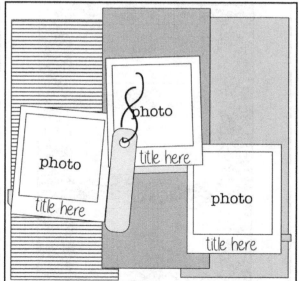

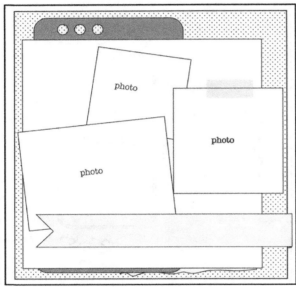

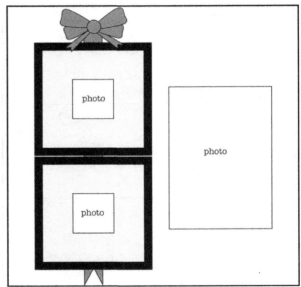

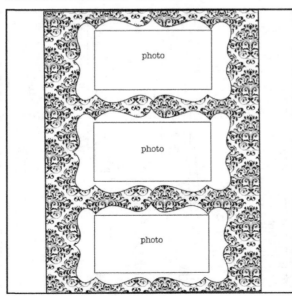

photo

photo

photo

Title Here

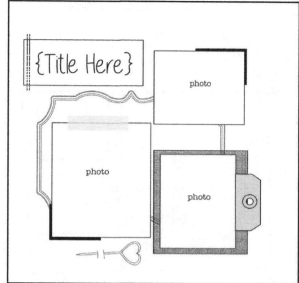

{Title Here}

photo

photo

photo

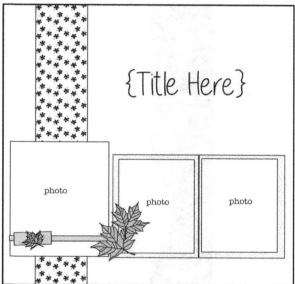

{Title Here}

photo

photo

photo

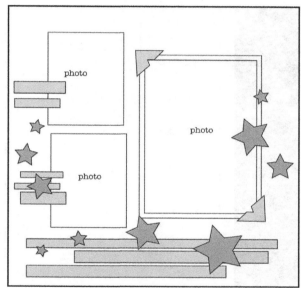

photo

photo

photo

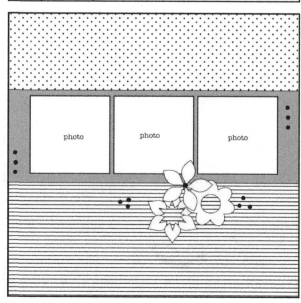

photo

photo

photo

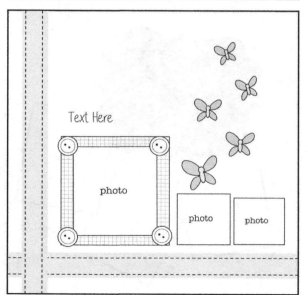

Text Here

photo

photo

photo

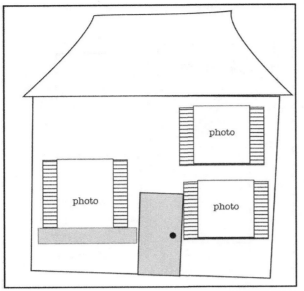

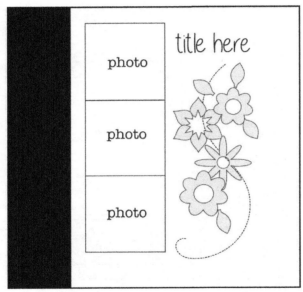

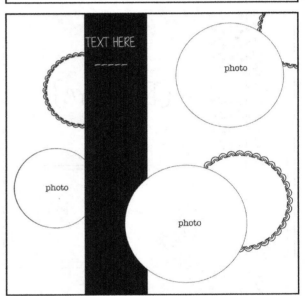

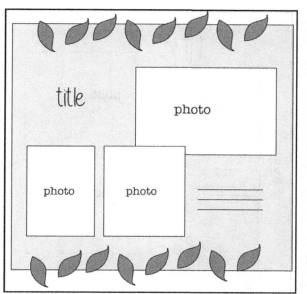

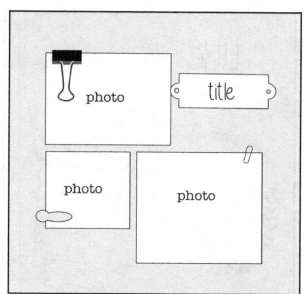

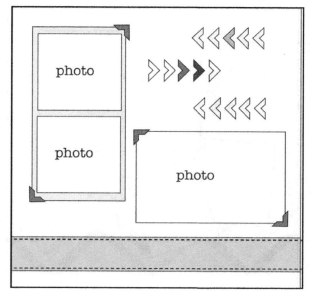

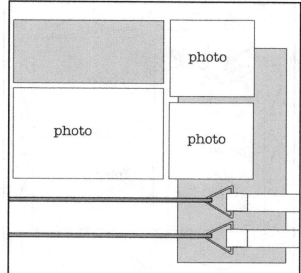

58

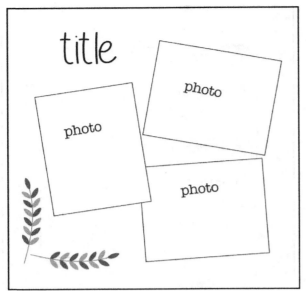

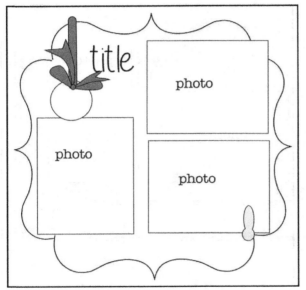

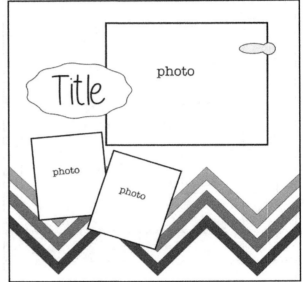

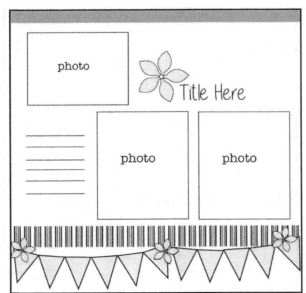

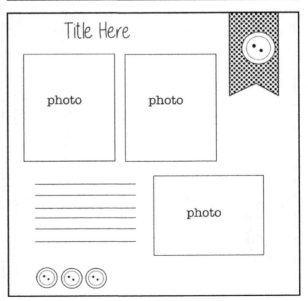

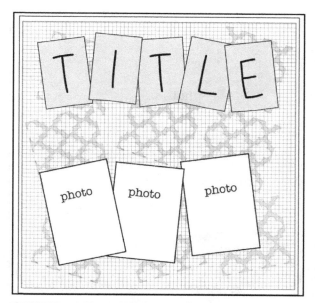

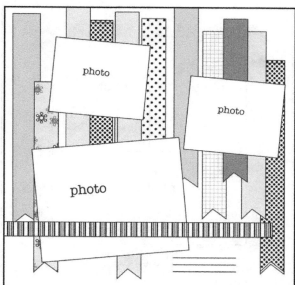

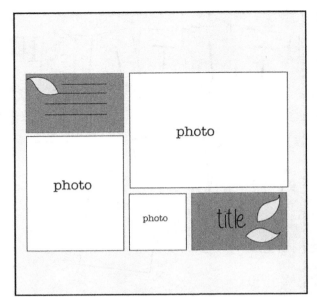

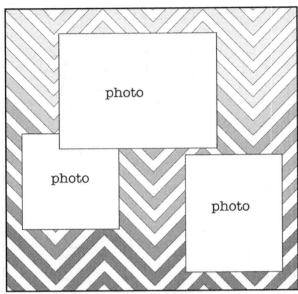

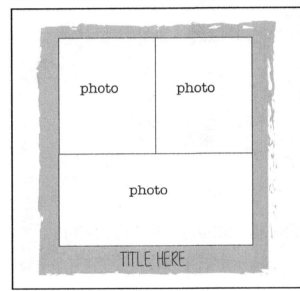

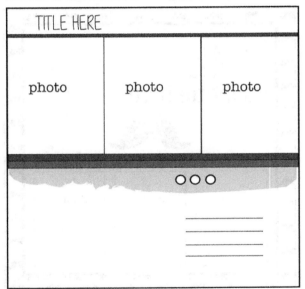

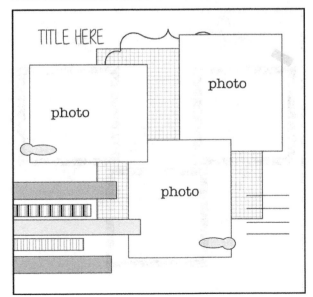

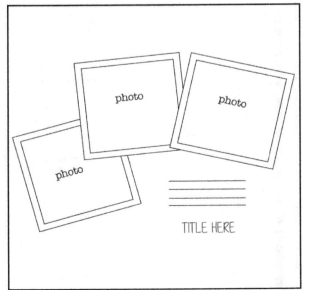

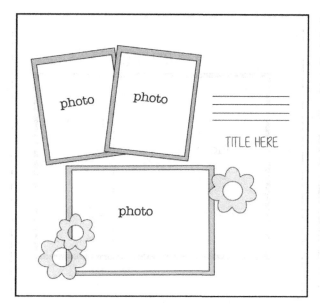

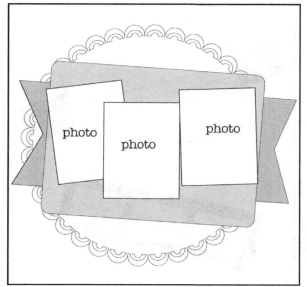

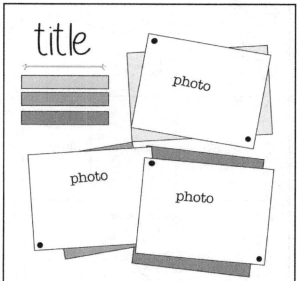

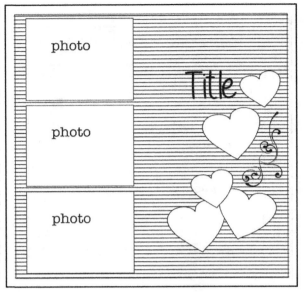

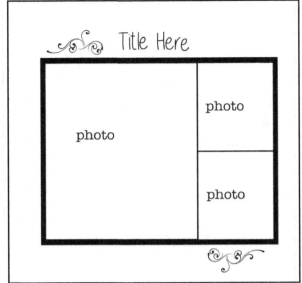

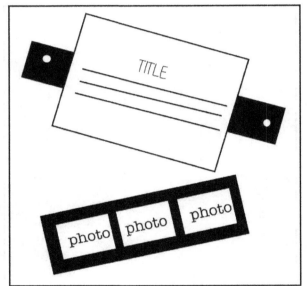

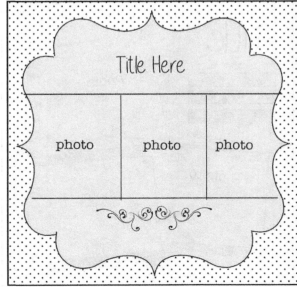

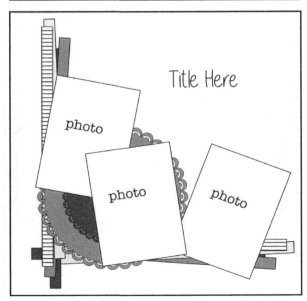

63

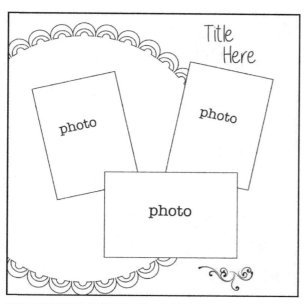

Title Here

photo

photo

photo

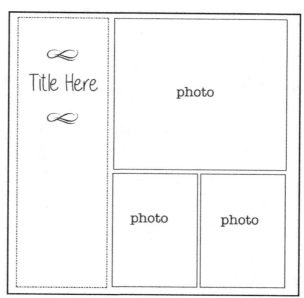

Title Here

photo

photo

photo

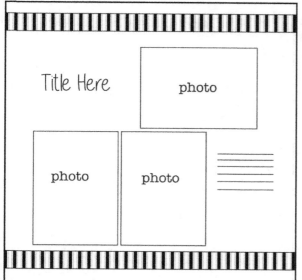

Title Here

photo

photo

photo

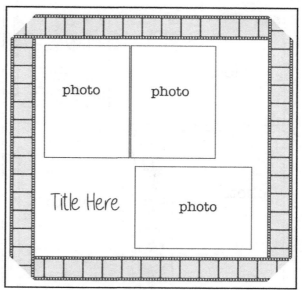

photo

photo

Title Here

photo

photo

photo

photo

Title Here

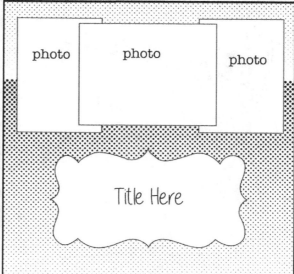

photo

photo

photo

Title Here

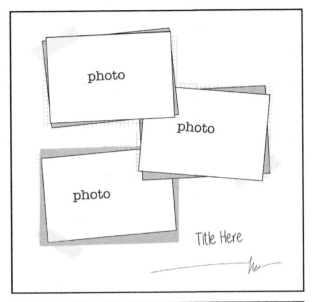

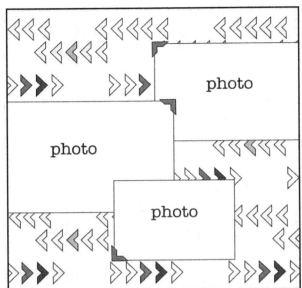

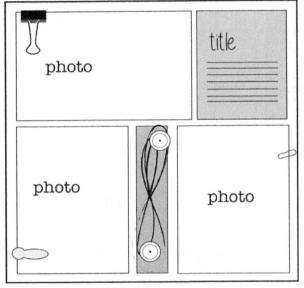

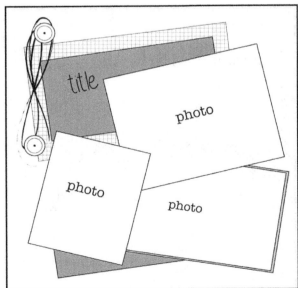

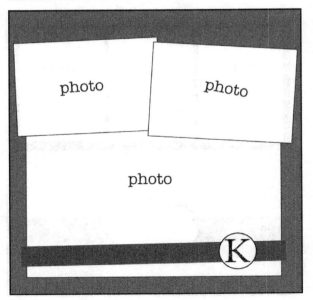

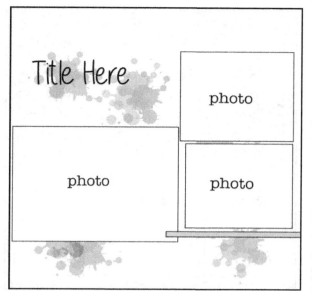

Title Here

photo

photo

photo

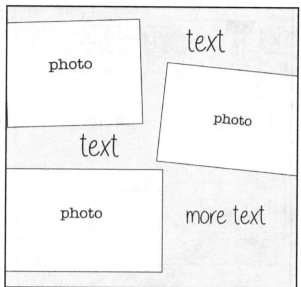

text

photo

photo

text

photo

more text

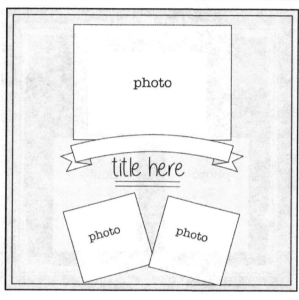

photo

title here

photo

photo

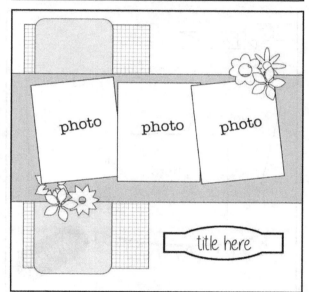

photo

photo

photo

title here

photo

title here }

photo

photo

photo

title here

photo

photo

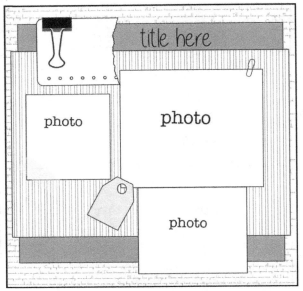

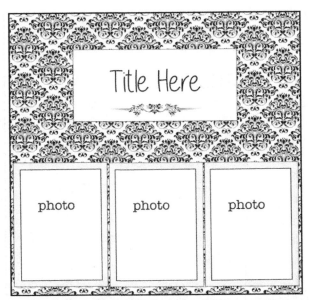

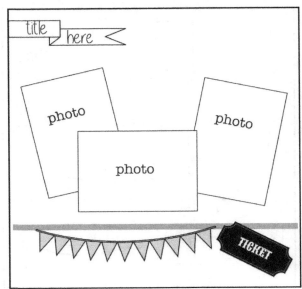

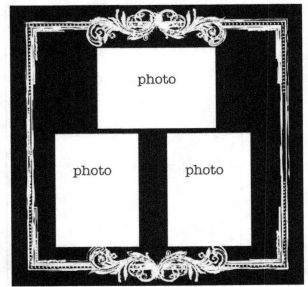

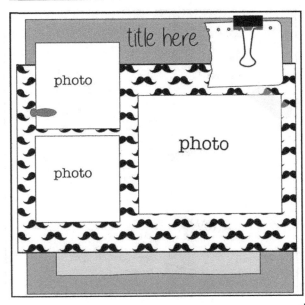

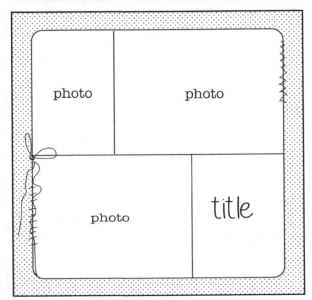

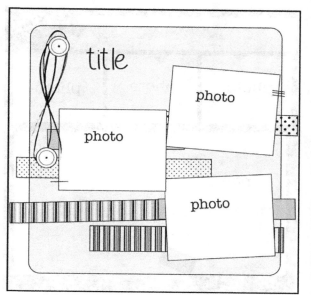

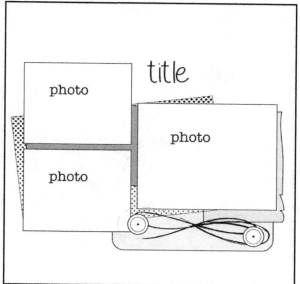

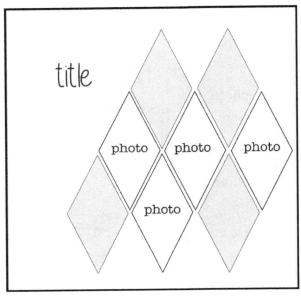

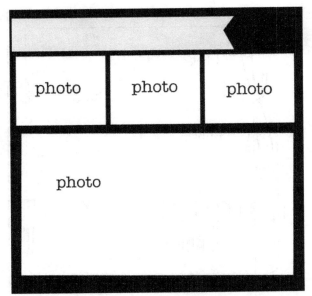

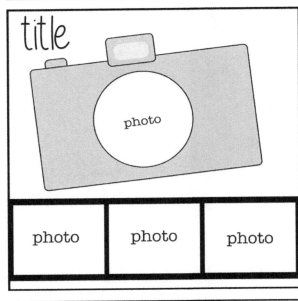

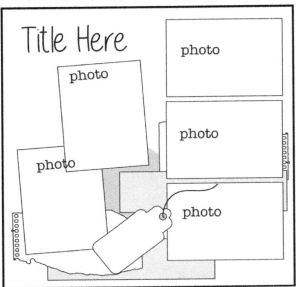

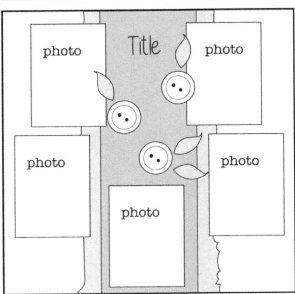

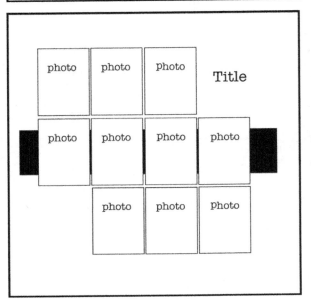

69

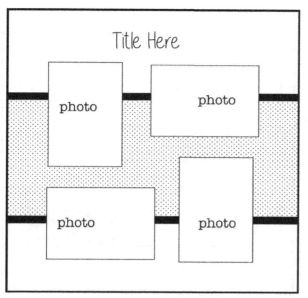

Title Here

photo

photo

photo

photo

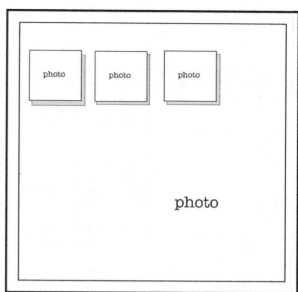

photo

photo

photo

photo

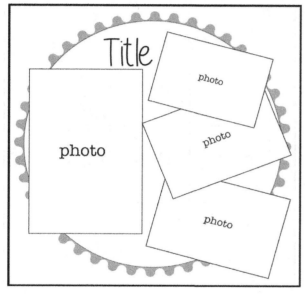

Title

photo

photo

photo

photo

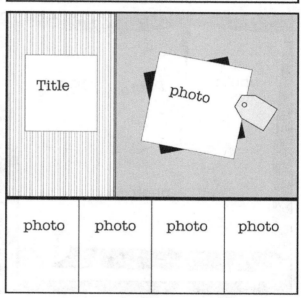

Title

photo

photo   photo   photo   photo

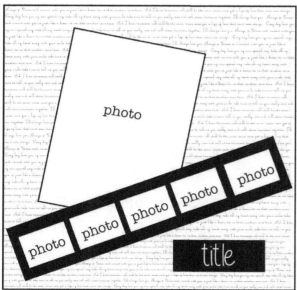

photo

photo   photo   photo   photo   photo

title

TITLE

photo

photo

photo

photo

photo

photo

70

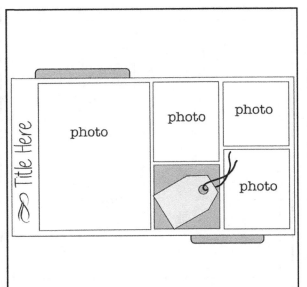

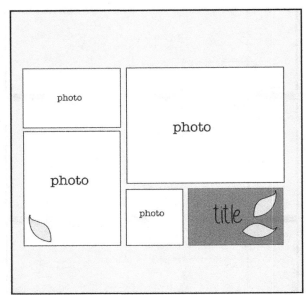

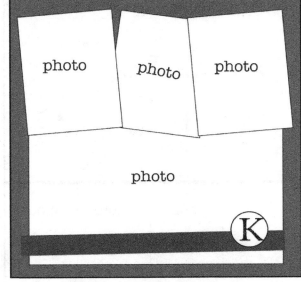

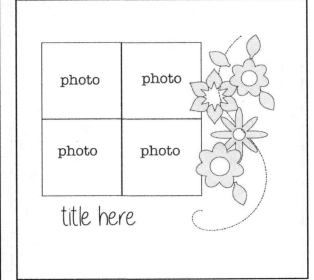

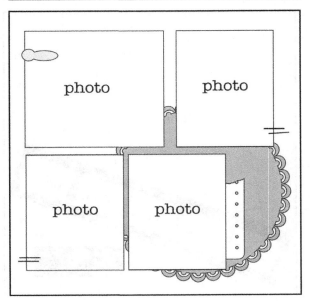

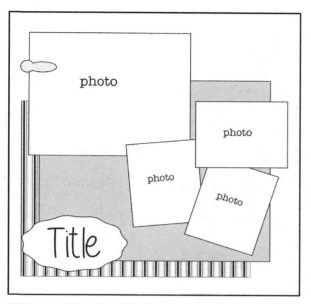

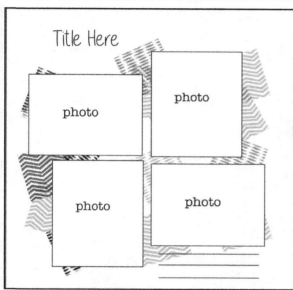

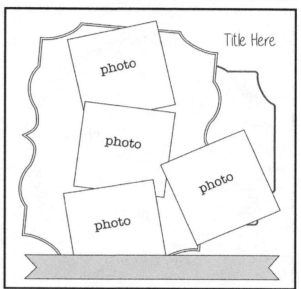

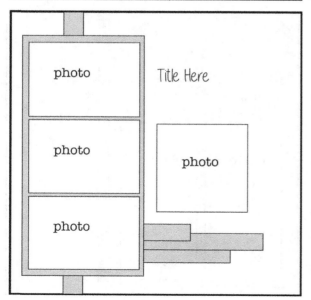

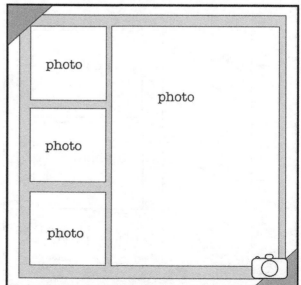

72

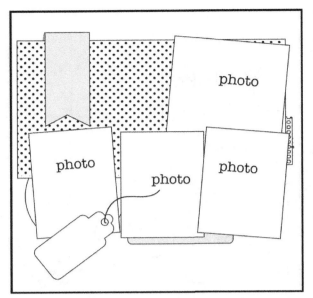

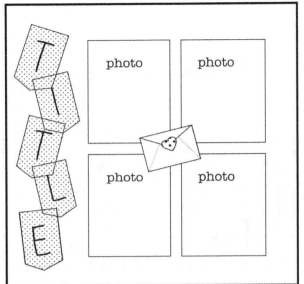

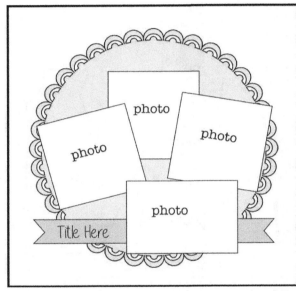

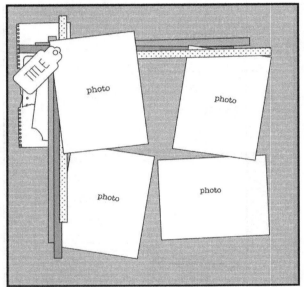

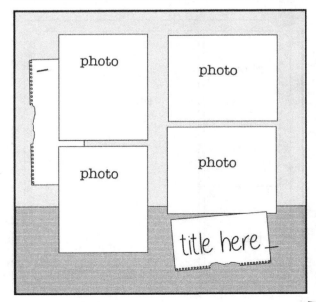

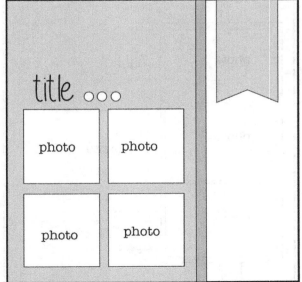

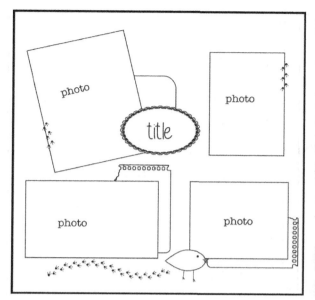

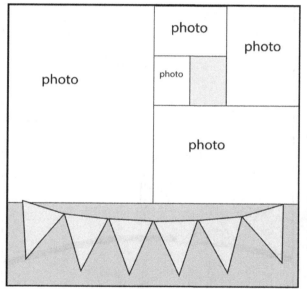

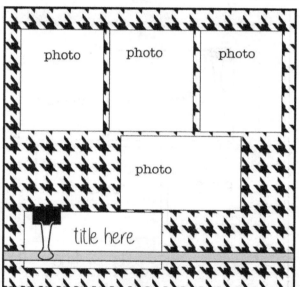

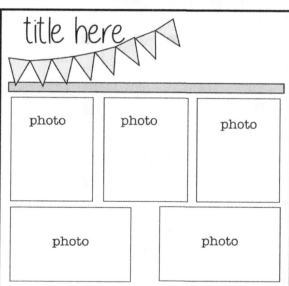

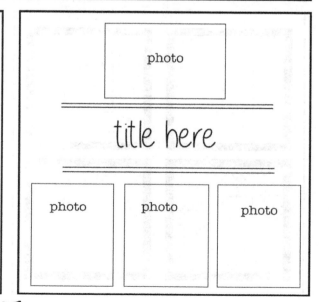

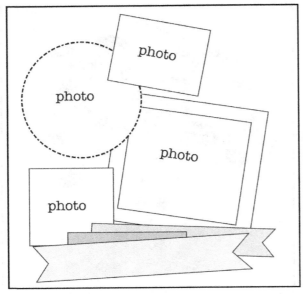

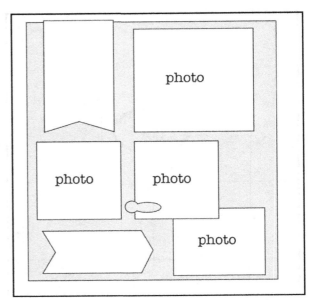

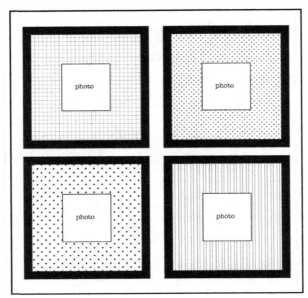

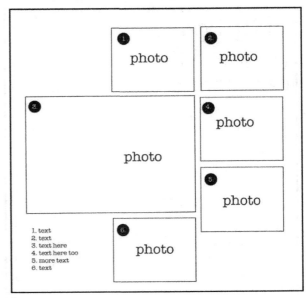

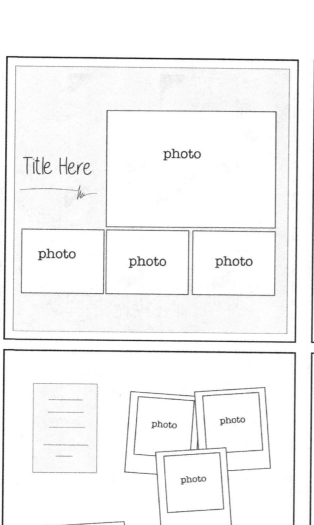

Title Here

photo

photo

photo

photo

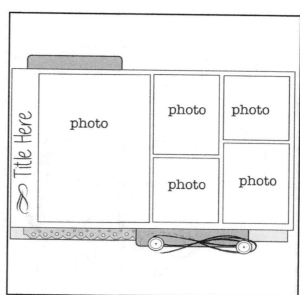

Title Here

photo

photo

photo

photo

photo

photo

photo

photo

photo

title here

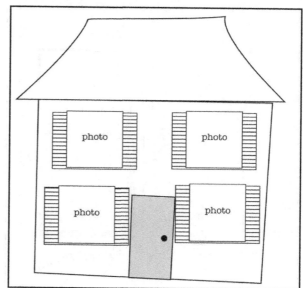

photo

photo

photo

photo

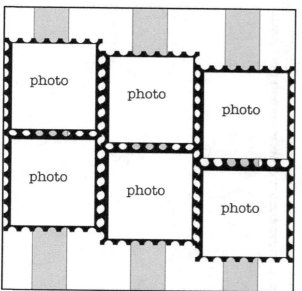

photo

photo

photo

photo

photo

photo

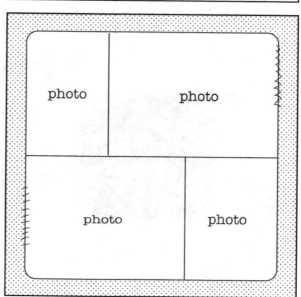

photo

photo

photo

photo

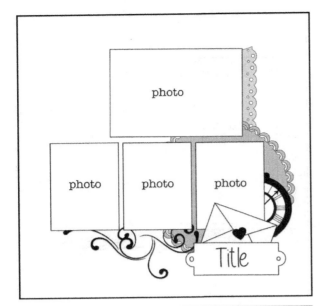

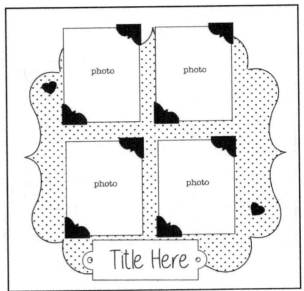

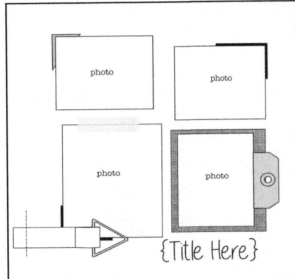

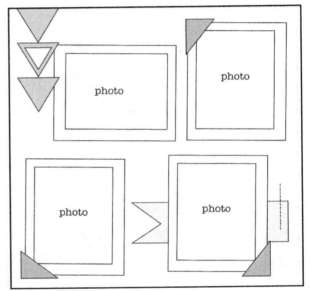

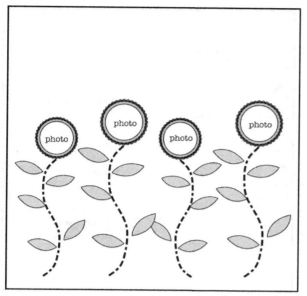

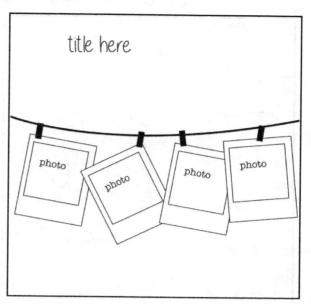

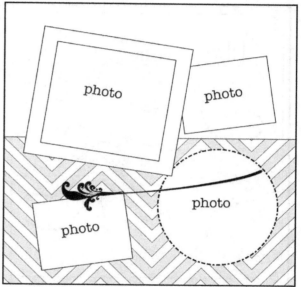

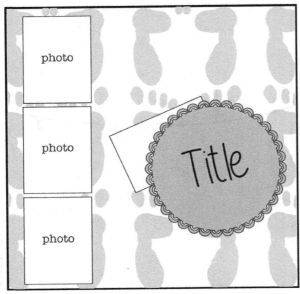

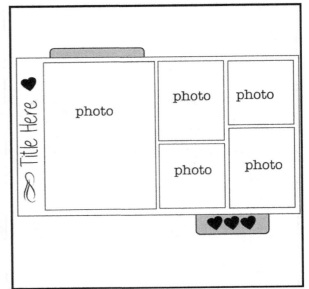

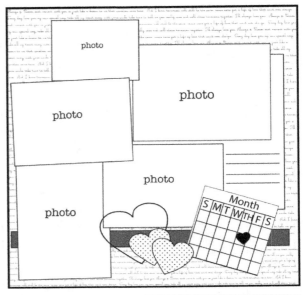

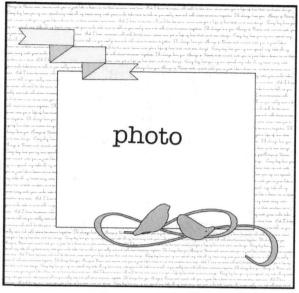

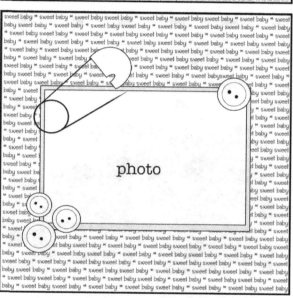

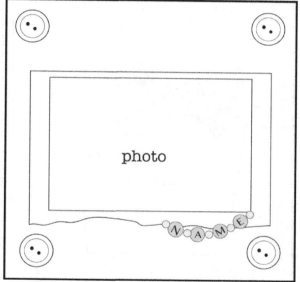

Merry Christmas

title here

title here

HAPPY 3RD BIRTHDAY

HAPPY BIRTHDAY!

Happy Birthday!!

Happy Birthday to You!

photo

photo

TITLE

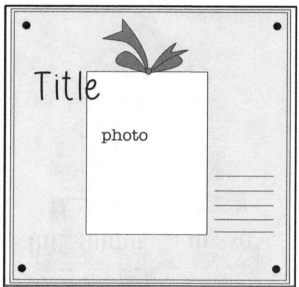

Title

photo

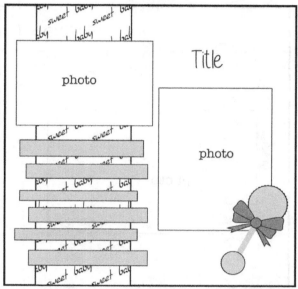

photo

Title

photo

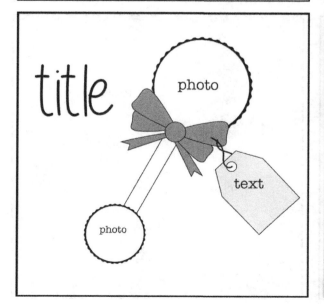

title

photo

text

photo

NOEL

photo

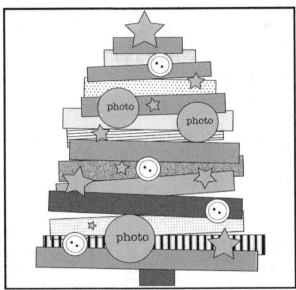

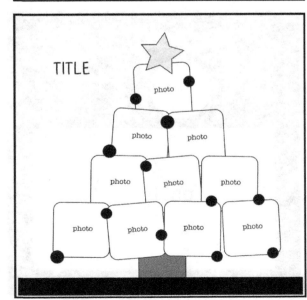

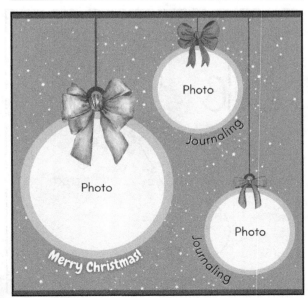

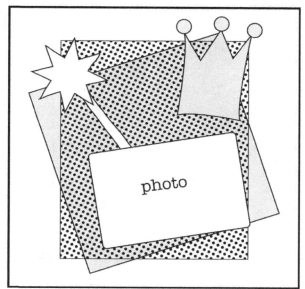

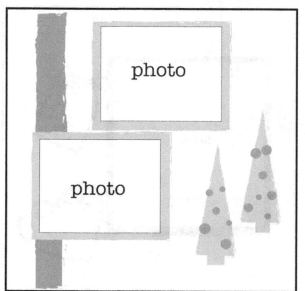

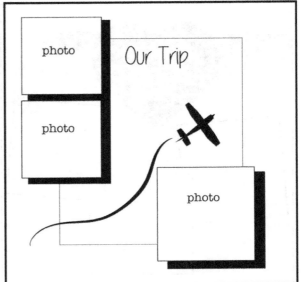

Our Trip

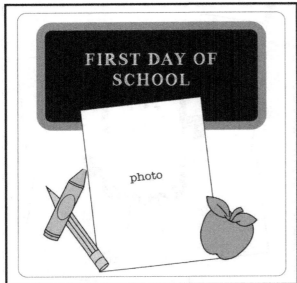

FIRST DAY OF SCHOOL

Text Here

Text Here

Title

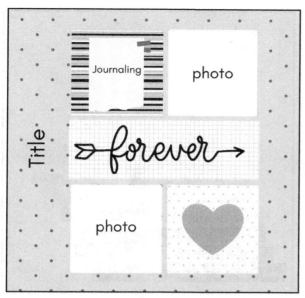

Title

Journaling

photo

forever

photo

Grandma's Favorite
(sshhhhh)

photo

photo

photo

OXOXOXO OXOXOXO OXOXOXO OXOXOXO OXOXOXO OXOXOXO OXOXO

photo

photo

photo

photo

photo

title here

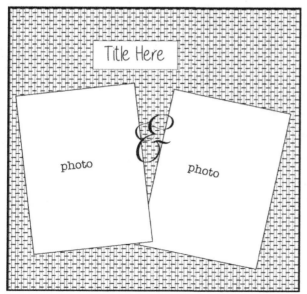

Title Here

photo

&

photo

title

photo

photo

photo

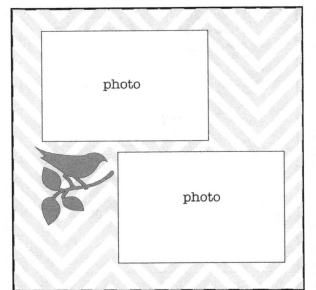

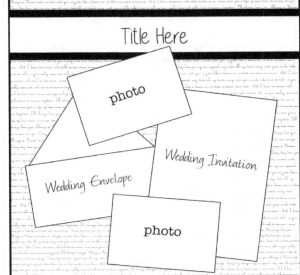

Double Page Sketches

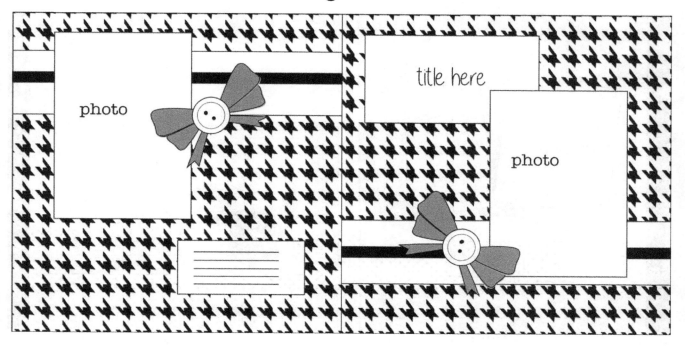

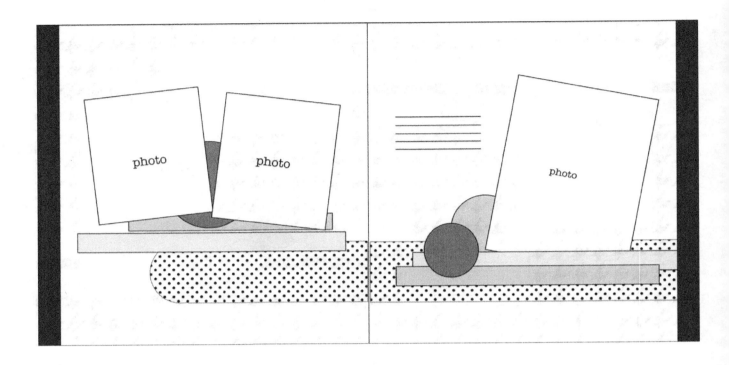

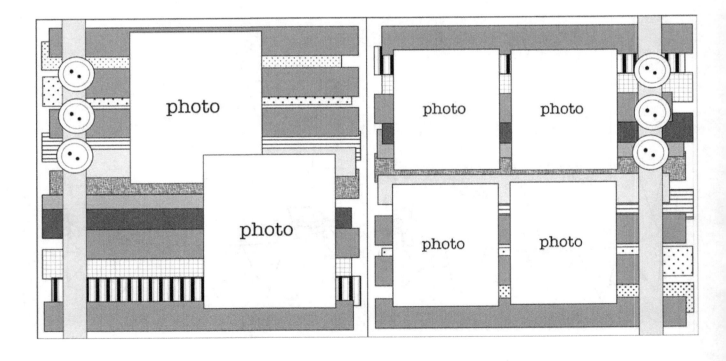

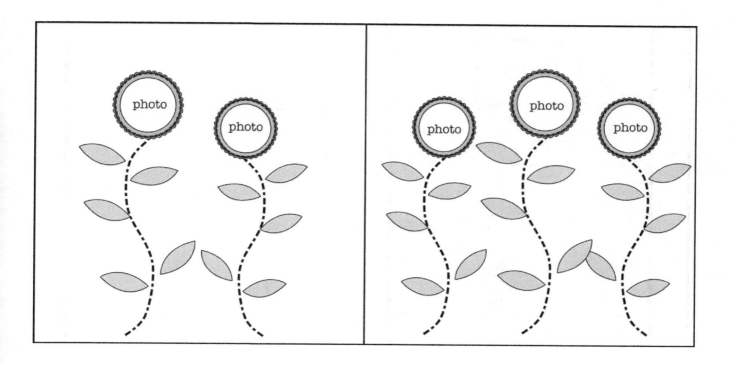

Title Here

photo

photo

Title Here

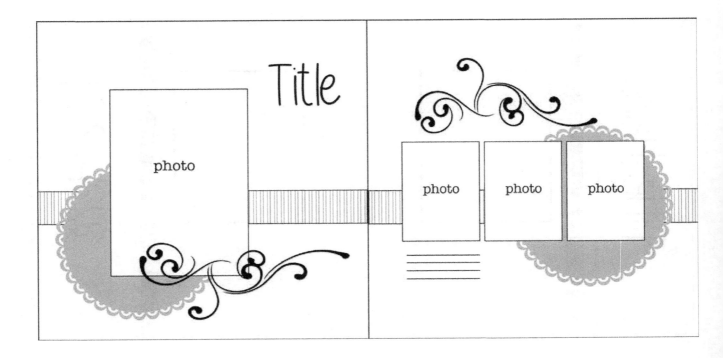

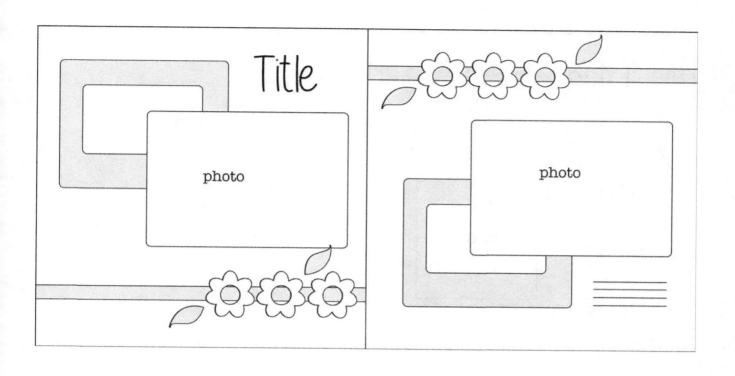

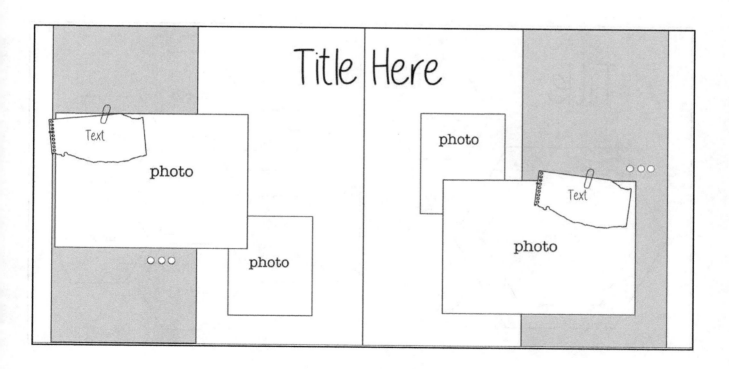

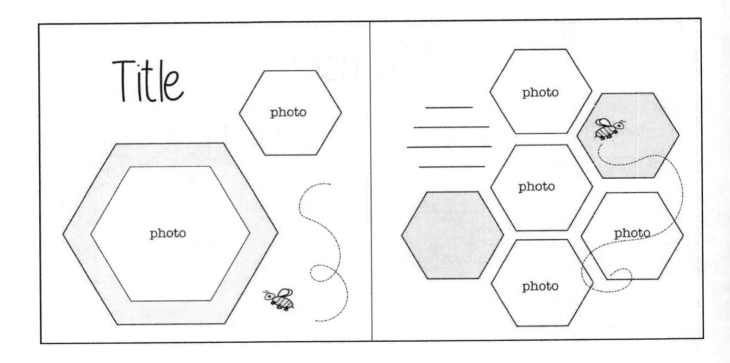

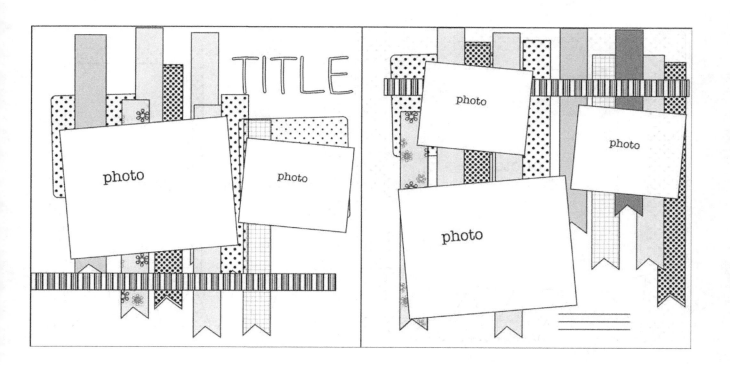

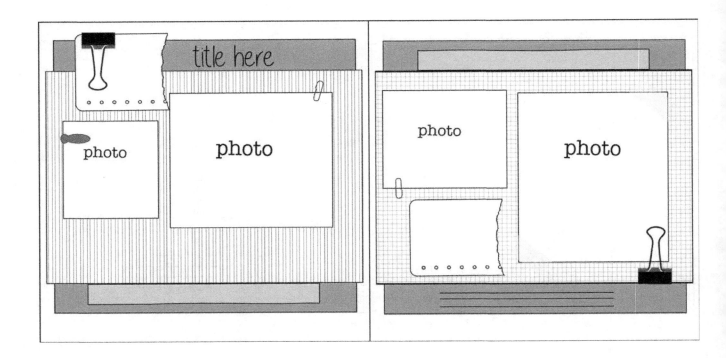

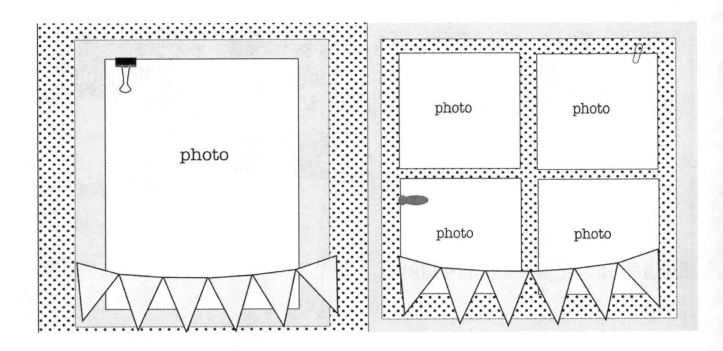

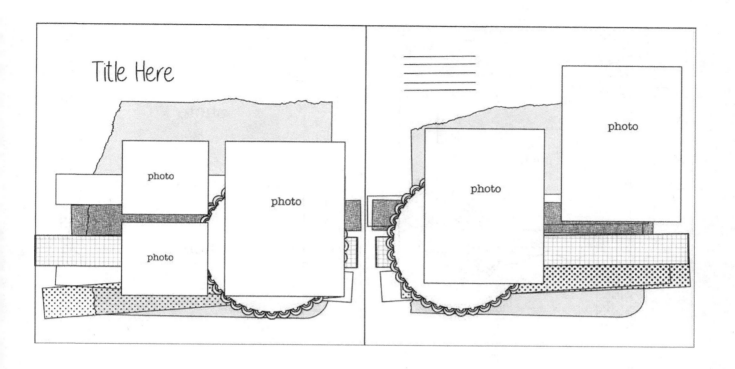

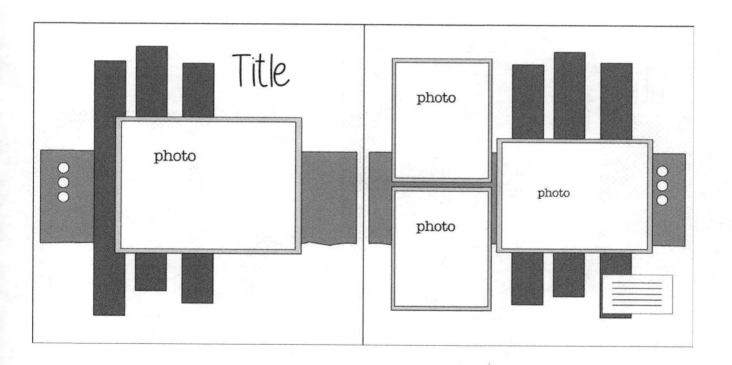

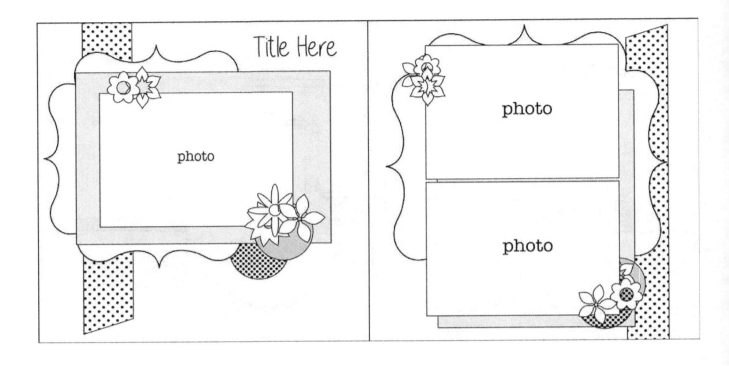

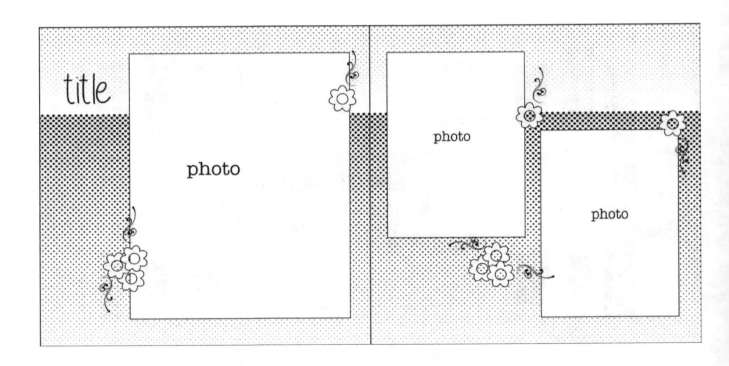

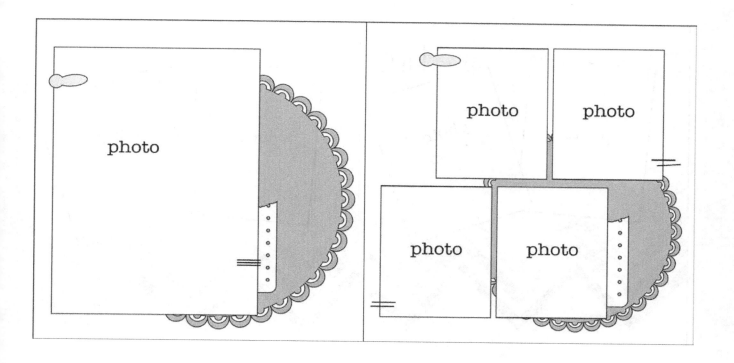

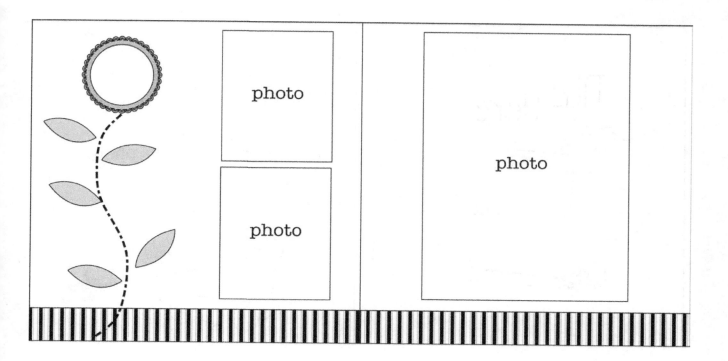

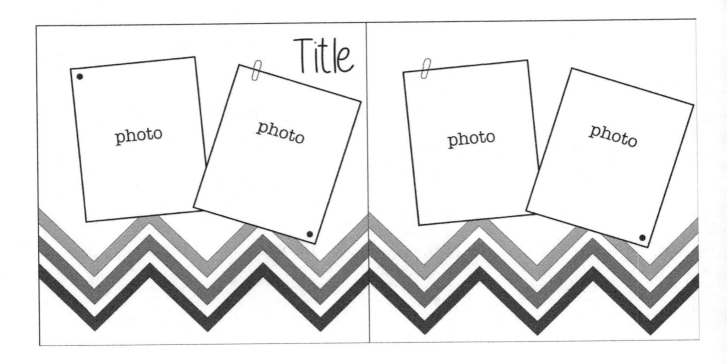

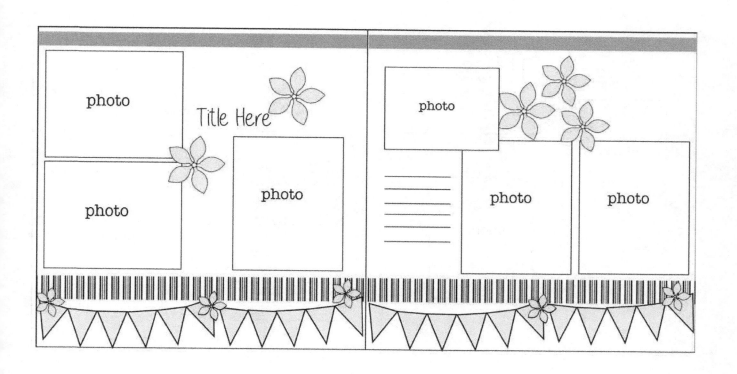

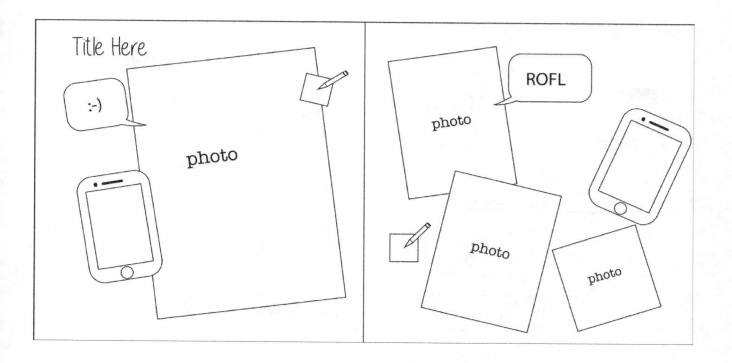

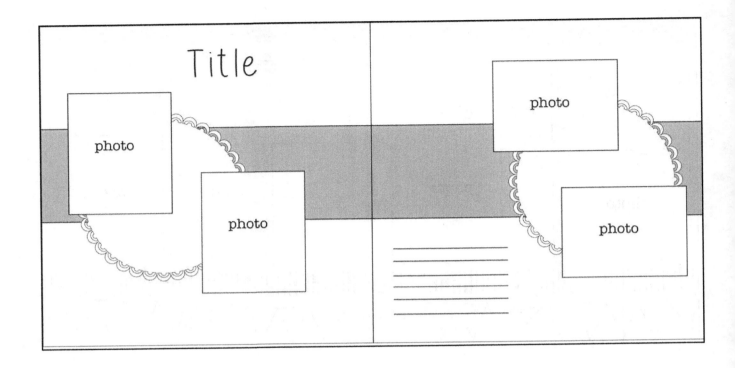

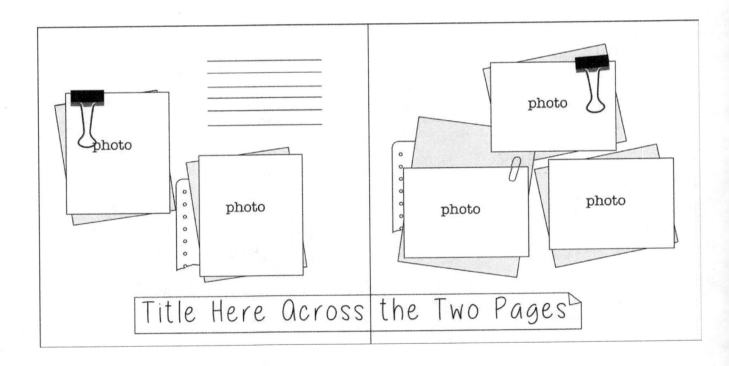

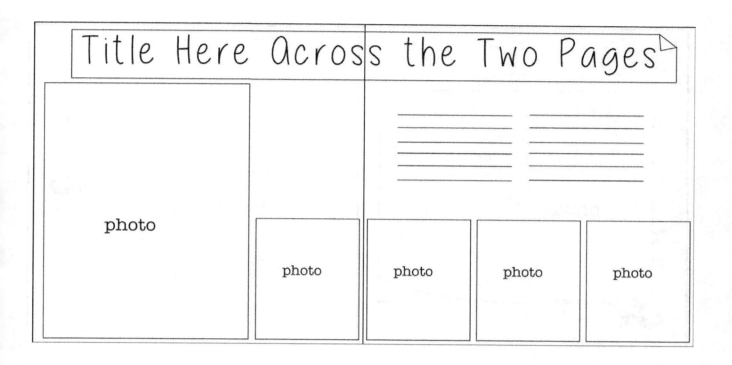

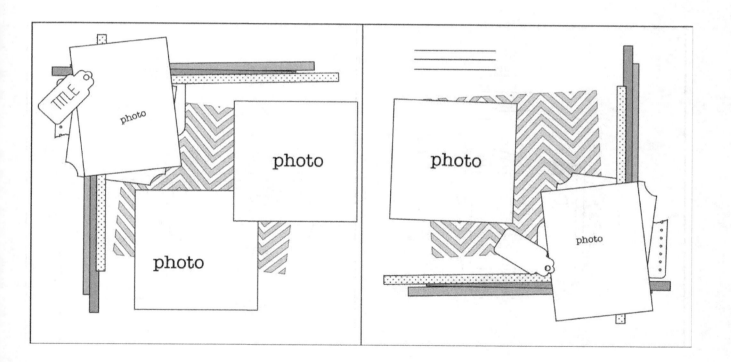

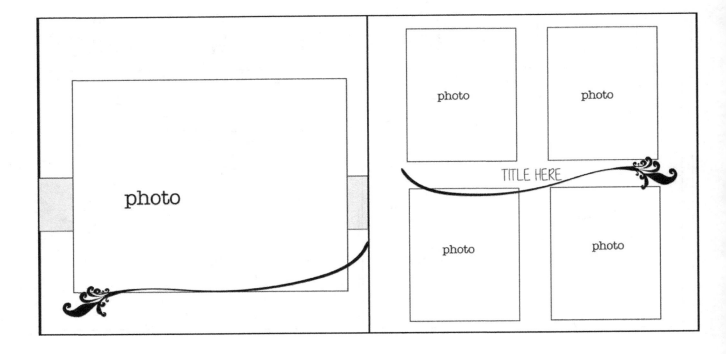

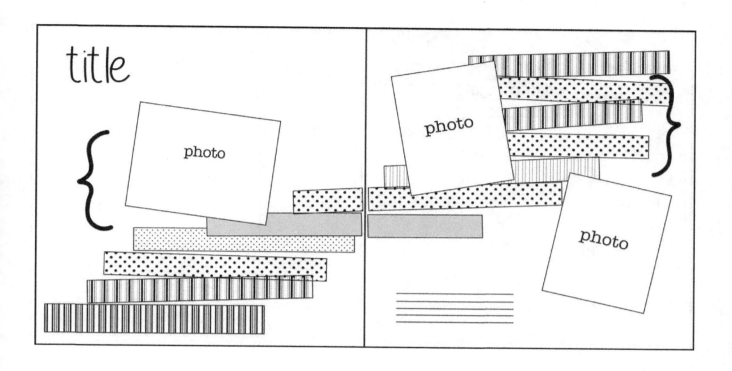

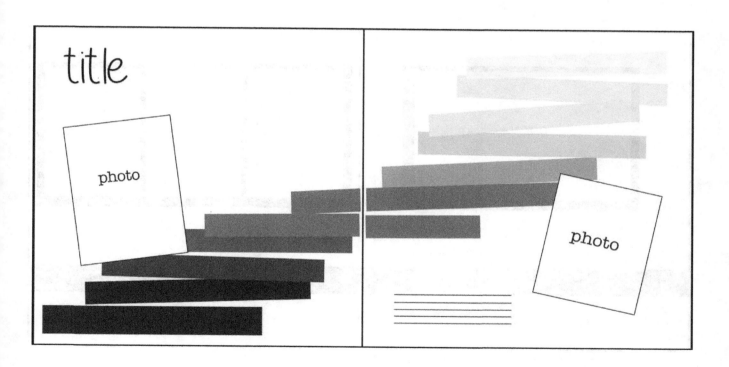

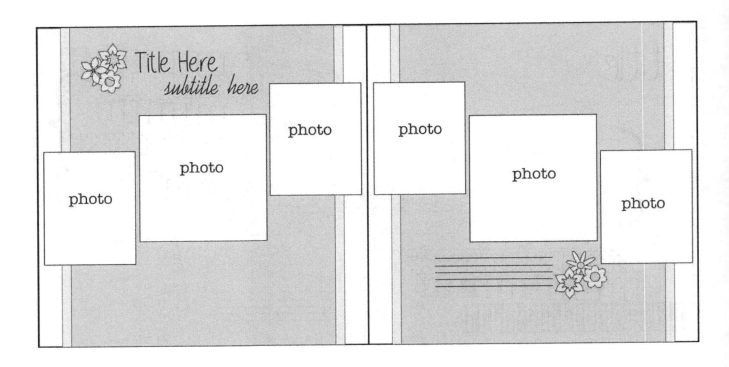

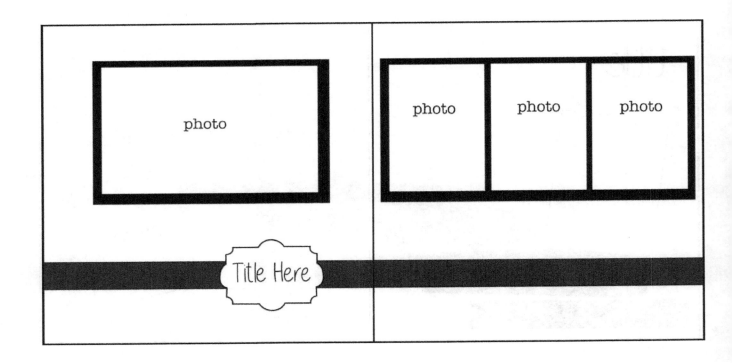

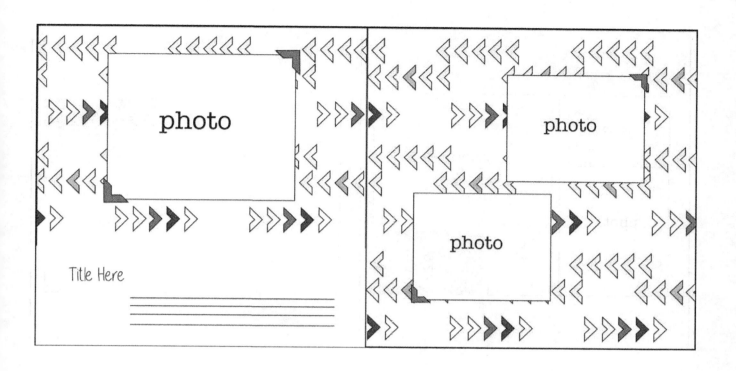

photo

Title Here

photo

photo

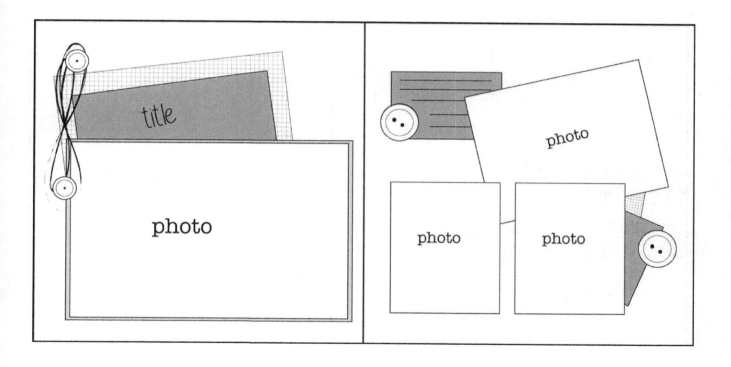

title

photo

photo

photo

photo

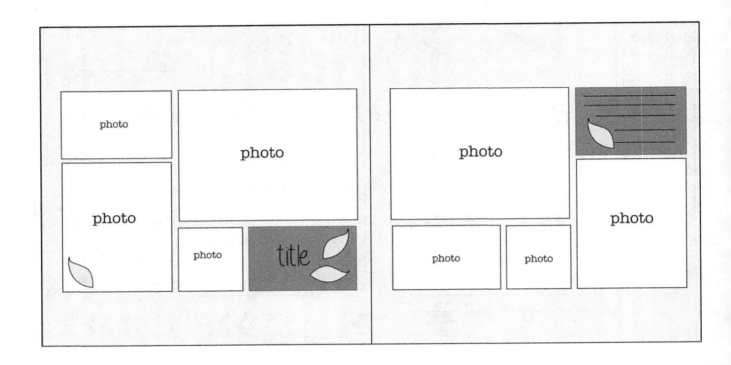

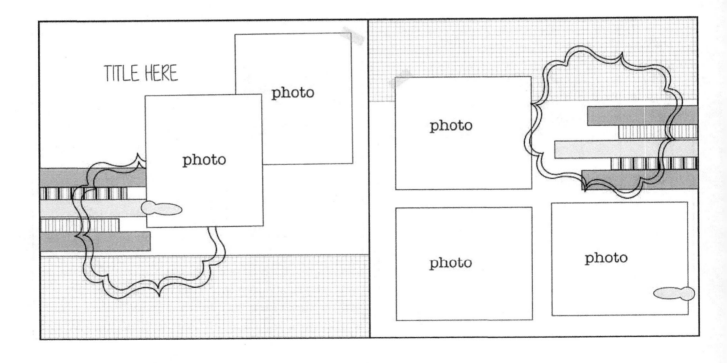

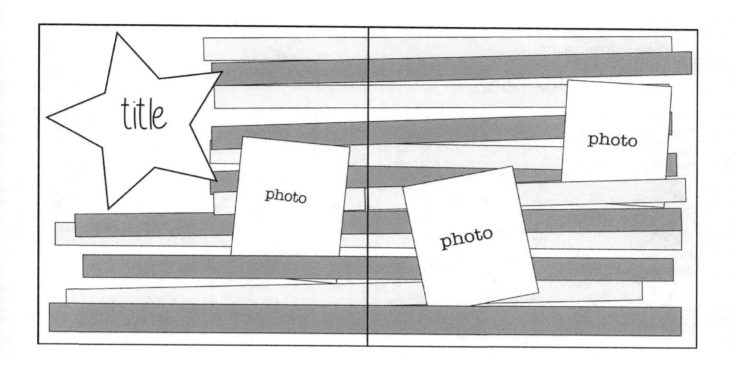

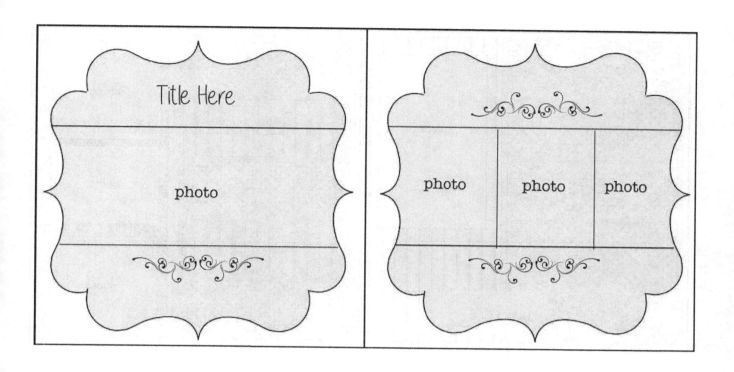

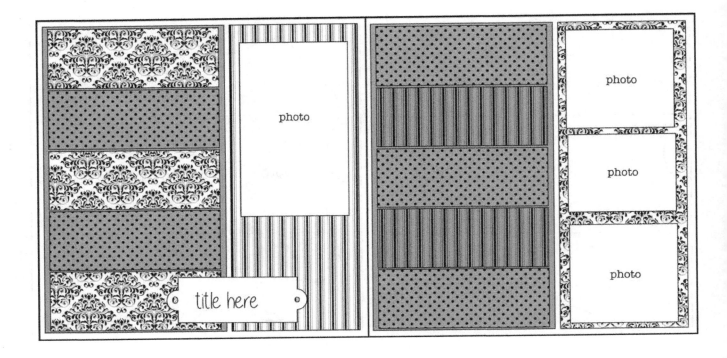

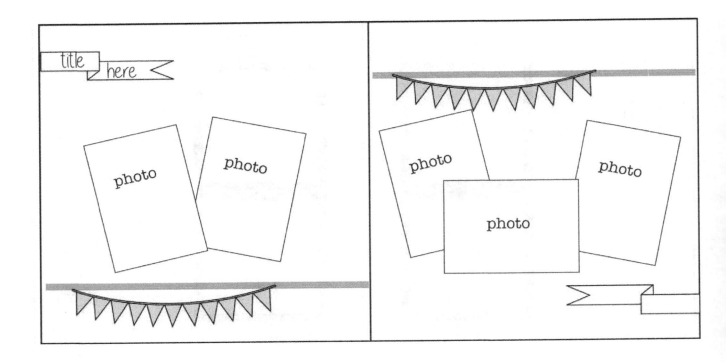

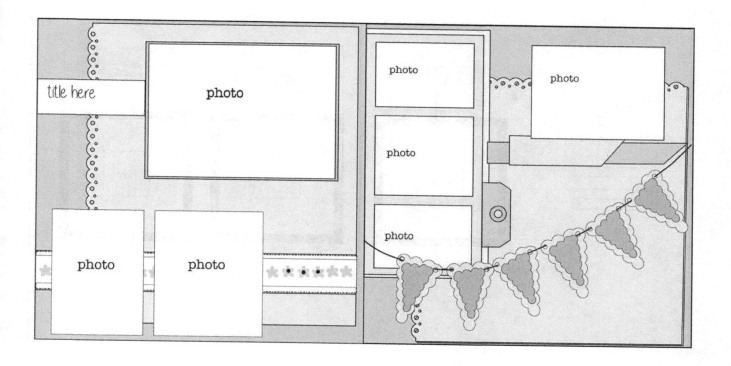

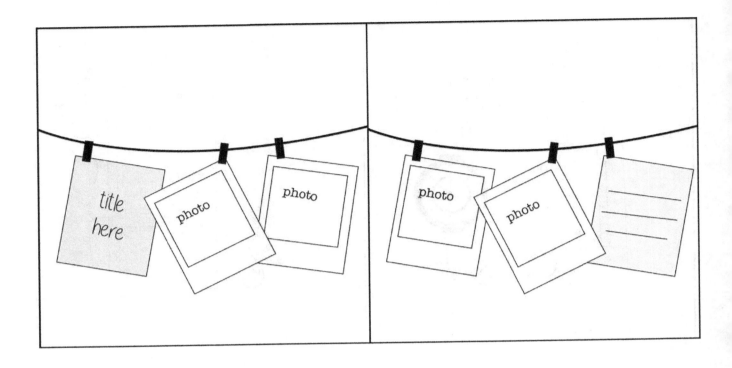

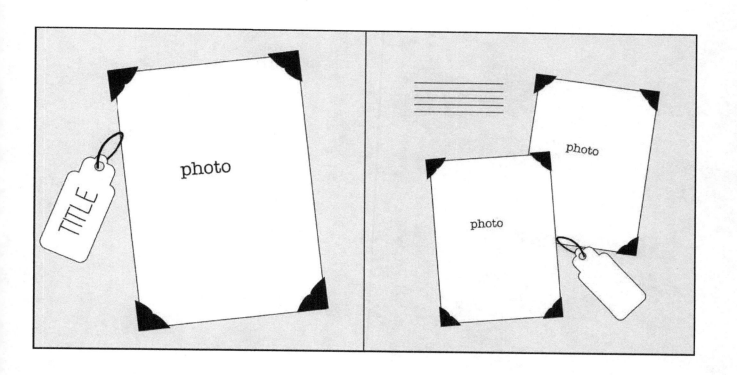

Made in the USA
Monee, IL
21 April 2025

16186952R00063